THE COLLECTOR'S GUIDE TO
ANTIQUE
FISHING TACKLE

THE COLLECTOR'S GUIDE TO
ANTIQUE
FISHING TACKLE

RODS • REELS • LURES • DECOYS • ART & ACCESSORIES • GUIDELINES

SILVIO CALABI

All photography, unless otherwise credited: Martin Sadofsky

Publishing Director: Frank Oppel
Editorial Director: Tony Meisel
Design Director: Carmela Pereira
Editor: Theresa Koziol
Composition: Meadowcomp Ltd..
Origination: Regent Publishing Services Ltd.
Printing: Leefung-Asco Printers Ltd.

Manufactured in Hong Kong
ISBN: 1-55521-525-4

CONTENTS

INTRODUCTION 7

RODS 9

REELS 51

LURES 99

DECOYS 147

ART & ACCESSORIES 171

COLLECTOR'S GUIDELINES 211

BIBLIOGRAPHY 220

INDEX 223

ACKNOWLEDGEMENTS

Many people contributed to this book. The author and the publisher would especially like to thank Lee and Joan Wulff; Len Codella and Tom Dorsey, of the Thomas & Thomas Rod Company, Turners Falls, Massachusetts; Bill Hunter, of Hunter's Angling Supplies, New Boston, New Hampshire; Jim Butler, of *Rod & Reel* Magazine; and Martin and Roberta Sadofsky.

Special thanks go to Richard Oliver, Bob Lang, and Susan Blaisdell of the RWO Gallery, Kennebunk, Maine, America's leading fishing-tackle auctioneers. They opened their gallery and warehouse for photography and provided significant insight into current trends in tackle collecting and investing.

INTRODUCTION

FISHING EQUIPMENT has hardly changed over the centuries. The earliest rods were saplings or tree branches; the earliest reels simple storage devices that line was wound around; the first terminal tackle was likely bits of food, feathers or fur impaled on a hook or simply tied to the line. Any of these things, in their simplest form, is still available today, down to the 14 foot natural cane pole with string, float and hook fixed to one end. A fisherman of Izaak Walton's time—or even earlier—would recognize it in an instant, and be able to put it to good use immediately. He might pause over a red-and-white plastic bobber or a modern tempered-steel, angled-shank bait hook, but only in admiration. He'd string up an angleworm, doughball or chunk of overripe cheese and head for the water, and by the time he got there he probably would have figured out how to slide the bobber up and down the line.

(That line might impress him with its slender diameter and smooth, even finish, but he'd be comforted by its familiar braided construction. He would shake his head in pleasure over its tensile strength, long life and resistance to rotting, but that would come only after a few days. The word "Dacron" wouldn't mean a thing to him; if he was particularly religious, he might think it one of the 666 names of Beelzebub.)

If this angler from the 16th or 17th century parked himself under a tree on the bank of an Alabama lake, pretty soon he'd be frightened out of his wits by a gleaming bass boat roaring past at high speed. Seeing the visitor's homespun clothing and odd hat, the moderns—embodiments of Southern hospitality, after all—would stop to exchange pleasantries. (And as fishermen they'd want to know how he was doing and what he was catching 'em on, too.) Once over his fright, and with a Lonestar longneck fresh from the cooler clutched in one hand, Izaak's kin might step aboard the boat for a tour. Again, there would be little in fishing tackle that he'd fail to recognize or understand in short order. Leaving off the mysteries of internal combustion, on-board refrigeration, recorded music and the like, only the electronic fish finder would throw him. And that goes for a lot of contemporary anglers too.

Likewise, the modern fisherman could step back to any time in sportfishing history and rapidly become adept with the then-current state of angling technology. While materials and techniques have evolved significantly, the basics are the same. Fish and their waters haven't changed, and we still go after them and into them in much the same way.

This goes a long way in explaining the strong, er, lure that elderly fishing tackle has for so many fishermen. No matter its age, origin, design or construction, the antique rod or reel–or lure, landing net, creel, fly box, knife–is familiar.

The comfort level is high. We understand it. Understanding it, we are free to admire the ingenuity, craftsmanship and artistic talent that went into it. It speaks to us of other times and people who were also engaged in something that we love.

RODS

FISHING RODS today are simultaneously the simplest and sometimes the most sophisticated of tools (toys?). What could be plainer than a stick to increase our reach from bank or boat to where the fish are? And yet few hand tools are more technologically complex than the modern hollow-section, progressive action, multipiece casting rod made from high Modulus synthetic fibers wrapped in precise configuration. On the one side we have a stone age implement; on the other, a technical marvel whose engineering, materials and construction methods were borrowed directly from air- and space craft.

Of particular interest to collectors, naturally, are the generations of fishing rods that come inbetween, chronologically and technologically. A stick is just a stick, and it's going to be difficult to prove that *this* stick is the very one shown in that famous ancient Egyptian fresco that seems to depict fishing with a rod and a feathered lure. And today's hollow graphite technical marvel commands no respect as a collectible either–it is too new, too state of the art, too much a product of automation, and a hundred thousand copies are racked neatly at tackle shops nationwide. As connoisseurs, collectors and critics of fishing tackle, we favor the rods that fall between these extremes, from approximately the 17th century to the present, for not all today's rods come hot and dripping with epoxy from huge curing ovens. Along with the possibility of being historically significant, the rods of this vintage combine in varying degrees both hand craftsmanship and superb function. (The former is lacking in current mass-produced rods; the latter itch was hardly scratched when rods were still in the longer reach-over-the-water stage of development.)

Rods that simply extend the fisherman's arm, as opposed to casting farther than their own length, are for dapping–gingerly placing a lure on the water directly over a fish, or where a feeding fish will find it. ("Lure" here means whatever the fish is meant to eat, be it natural bait, an artificial fly or a hardbodied manmade lure.) This gentle sport is likely one of the very earliest kinds of rod-and-line fishing, but it is still practised in North America and Europe, and not just by children whose allowances haven't achieved parity with tackle prices. During the famous mayfly hatch on Ireland's Lough Corrib, local and visiting aficionados snatch trout by delicately skating artificial flies through the lake's surface film on ultrafine monofilament tied to poles 12 to 15 feet long. And along the shorelines of Southern ponds, a dapping rod can be a deadly tool for snaking crappies out from beneath their protective brushy covers, in water where a casting-rod presentation would be impossible.

By today's standards, fishing rod development proceeded slowly in the 16th, 17th and 18th centuries, and was hampered far more by the physical limits of the available raw materials than by any ignorance of fish or fishing on the part of the rod makers.

Anyone who wades through the antique vocabulary and grammar of old "fysshnge" manuscripts can't help but be impressed by the currency of the information about tackle and fishing. Barring common biological or botanical misconceptions, that is: A medieval poem called *Piers of Fulham*, unearthed by scholar Richard Hoffmann in 1985, actually scolds anglers who keep small fish that haven't reached their full growth, and this was in the 13th century. The notion that it was the big breeding stock that should be let go instead didn't take root for another 600 years.

The 17th century angler chose his rod based on the water to be fished: Tiny meadow brooks called for relatively light rods that could be used with one hand, while lakes or large rivers—or large fish—prompted fishermen to use cumbersome poles as long as 21 feet. These could be wielded only with both hands, and with great difficulty at that, for they were generally solid along much of their length, for strength. The butt diameter was commonly well over an inch, and the weight might be two pounds or more, much of it far above the fisherman's hands. "Balanced" tackle as we know it was still many generations away.

(Dr. James Henshall's revolutionary wooden "bait rod" for bass fishing—made, incidentally, by The Orvis Company—in the 1880s was eight feet three inches long, and it was well complemented by the Kentucky baitcasting reels of its day. Downright modern was James Clark's "Chicago" rod of 1885, only six feet long.)

Rod length meant reach and, to some extent, lifting power. Because the line was attached to the rod tip, landing a fish meant hoisting it out of the water and onto shore. If the banks were brushy, or the fish was unusually large, or if the fisherman was in a skiff, he had to hand-over-hand the rod, feeding the butt out behind himself, until he could reach the tip and then the line and finally the fish itself. Hardly practical. Gaffs and landing nets were common, but an 18-foot rod and a five-foot net must have been difficult for one person to deal with, especially when a particularly large fish was tugging on the one and trying to avoid the other. Many early fishing scenes show pairs of fishermen, one on the rod, the other working the net.

Early improvement in fishing rods moved in step with improvements in lines and hooks. As lines, made of braided horsehair or vegetable fiber or, later, silk filaments, slowly became finer and stronger, and as hook wire also became more refined, anglers could fish smaller baits or flies on longer lines and still be reasonably assured of holding their fish. (Smaller fish, that is. As Col. Joe Bates points out in his superb *The Art of the Atlantic Salmon Fly*, before reels and running line were available an outsize fish such as a salmon could destroy in seconds a rod-and-line outfit that might have taken weeks to make. Upon hooking a salmon, it was not uncommon to toss the rod in the water and hope that all could be recovered undamaged when the fish got tired of towing it around.) Fishermen took advantage of this progression by flipping these ever longer lines farther and farther out onto the water, which let them not only reach more fish but also do so with less chance of spooking them. Another method, "blowline" fishing, was simply to let the wind take the line out, then drop the rod tip and the lure at the right instant. Of course, storing all this line and bringing the fish to hand then became more and more of a problem. One couldn't simply go on extending the handle of one's gaff or net. It was time to invent the winch, or reel–but that is another chapter . . . .

From earliest times fishermen have known that rods must be somewhat springy in order to protect the relatively delicate line by absorbing the shocks of struggling fish. Too rigid a rod tip makes it difficult to sense fishy activity at the hook and also interferes–from the angler's viewpoint–with the pleasant sensations of the struggle. And finally, rods have to be strong enough to resist breaking themselves. As this business of extending the range by flipping longer and longer fixed lines caught on, another prime requisite for a fishing rod came to the fore: It had to have an action, or "feel"–or flexural profile, if you prefer–that suited this job. Casting had been born; and, with it, the casting rod. Modern sportfishing was here.

(Historians may argue here over the word "sportfishing," as opposed to fishing for food or commerce. I'm referring just to fishing with a rod and line. As nets and trotlines had already been in wide use for millenia, and their efficiency for "commercial" fishing well established, I'm assuming that anyone in this period who chose to fish with a rod did so more for fun than the strict need to feed the family. Hence "sport" fishing.)

Already by the late 1600s there were commercial rod makers known to be at work in London and probably in Continental and colonial capitals as well, and it is highly likely that others preceeded them by many years. For their time, they were as versed in their art as any 20th century rod crafts-man, and they experimented and researched and invented and poked and prodded continually to im-prove their merchandise. As rods became longer, the problems of weight versus strength–not to men-tion storage and portability–became acute. The rod builders' answer was the multipiece fishing rod, which came apart into usually two or three sections. As the state of the art progressed, wooden rods of up to 12 or more pieces eventually appeared.

The first mention of multipiece rods that I am aware of is in the famous "Treatyse of Fysshnge wyth an Angle," a chapter of *The Boke of St. Albans*, published in 1496. The author, reputedly the legendary abbess Dame Juliana Berners, provides fairly detailed instructions for making a three-piece, two-section fly rod. (Whether professional rod makers were around yet or not, it was common until well into the 19th century for fishermen to build their own rods.) "She" recommends a tip made from black thorn spliced onto hazel, both smoothly tapered and finished to provide a sensitive action–and also to store neatly in the hollow rod butt made of seasoned ash! As the book was probably passing on the fishing wisdom of the day, rather than blazing new trails in tackle and technique, hollow-section rods may have been around for some time already.

As most such developments are, this was both a blessing and a curse.

It was all well and good to saw a long rod into shorter pieces, or try to assemble one from smaller sections. The difficulty was that these pieces had to be joined together, quickly and infallibly, and then disassembled afterward with equal ease. Furthermore, these joints could not be so stiff, heavy, long or otherwise "dead" as to interrupt the rod's action. Fishing was about to take another great step forward.

A drawing from the "Treatise" of the two-piece rod shows butt and tip mated together with an iron reinforcing ring over the joint. It looks somewhat like a modern sleeve ferrule. On that rod, likely only the tip flexed. Other early joints were actually splines or splices, rather than sleeves: The end of each rod section was cut flat on a long taper; two of these flats were mated up and lashed together as securely as possible with cords or leather thongs. This isn't quite as ridiculous as it sounds. Such a splice joint, well made, is reasonably strong, and several British makers still offer them today. The few devotees of spliced joints claim nothing else provides such a smooth and uninterrupted rod action. (My guess is that most of them fish only their own ancestral rivers and live in castles whose towering ceilings and doors let them store their rods without ever having to break them down.)

It didn't take long—and in fact it may have happened almost simultaneously—for rod makers to come up with hollow sleeve-type joints of rolled tubes of brass, copper, silver or German silver (also known as nickel-silver) that slip together. Crude ferrules of the day had no metal male section at all; the fisherman just forced the wooden end of the upper section into a metal tube on the butt.

Some wonderful contraptions were invented, a few of which survive in production today, and there must be collectors who specialize in antique ferruling systems.

Around 1800 spike, or doweled, ferrules appeared. These had tapered male pins that probably did not hold very well in their female tubes. Late in that century, more sophisticated designs were developed to improve the holding power and "liveliness" of ferrules: Lock-fast ferrules have an internal dowel arrangement secured by some sort of external device. Many Hardy rods from Victorian times actually screw together; the plug and socket sections are slid into each other until a grooved finger on the outside of the male engages a coarse screw thread on the outside of the female, then you simply turn until snug. The thread draws the rod sections together. Other lock-fast ferrules featured a female sleeve with a right-angle notch cut in it, and a male plug with a mating pin or button protruding. These were slid together, the pin aligned in the notch, and then rotated to lock, like the bulb in a modern automotive light socket. Both types automatically squared up the line guides on each rod section, a minor convenience that today's non-locking ferrules don't provide.

For greater delicacy and improved rod action, ferrule walls were thinned and diameters were reduced. For improved holding, straight sections were added behind the tapered spike of the male, and then the spike was deleted entirely. By 1878 pioneering rod builder Hiram Leonard, a Maine man, had patented waterproof ferrules with split edges that allowed a smoother progression of flex from the rod into and through the ferrule. At the turn of the century the modern metal ferrule stood about as it is accepted today: simply a pair of stepped-diameter soldered nickel-silver (18 percent nickel-silver, to be exact) tubes that fit precisely together and hold by friction. Actually, there's nothing simple about it.

Traditionally, such ferrules are made in sizes that step up by a sixty-fourth of an inch (in outside diameter of the male plug). The size relates directly to weight and stiffness, and cane-rod builders today often classify their rods by length and ferrule. A 7 1/2-12, for example, is not a seven-foot six-inch rod for 12-weight line, as it would be for makers of graphite rods. It's a 7 1/2-footer with a size 12 ferrule; and, since only one ferrule size is mentioned, the rod must be a two-piece style. This rod might cast a 5-weight fly line. Recognizing that variety is the spice, the maker might also offer a 7 1/2-11 rod–the slimmer ferrule denoting a finer and less powerful rod, appropriate for maybe a #4 line. Similarly, a 7 1/2-13 would be a beefier rod for heavier use.

Ferrule diameters must be matched carefully to the rod blanks to keep the casting action alive. Eighteen percent nickel-silver flexes slightly, machines and solders well, and takes a handsome finish. The sleeves that fit over the ends of the cane sections are either finely notched or tapered in wall thickness. This lets the maker mold the metal tube to the (usually) hexagonal shape of the rod so there is no abrupt transition in either shape or stiffness. The male section is left slightly oversize, relative to the inside diameter of the female, until both halves are glued and pinned to their rod sections. Then the final, critical fitting begins. Working with a low-speed lathe and a dull file, the craftsman slowly and evenly reduces the male diameter, continually trying it in the female, until a perfect full-length friction fit is achieved. The tolerance is within a few ten-thousandths of an inch. The distinctive *snick* of a well-made ferrule being taken apart is as elegant a sound as the clunk of a Rolls-Royce door.

Inexpensive metal ferrules fit poorly–when you hold the rod near the ferrule and let it flex, you may hear or feel a click as the male rocks inside the female. Mass-produced metal ferrules, rare today except on mass-market children's outfits, were common on all sorts of rods in the first half of this century, and many were probably hand-fitted (as opposed to completely hand-made). They were usually of one-piece, drawn-tube construction; the male had a rounded end, the female a rolled edge. Many of these make the same metallic, vacuum-popping snick, but they are less integrated into their rod blanks and these rods are generally less valuable to the collector. A top-drawer handmade female ferrule normally has a reinforcing lip or welt that is soldered on, and an internal waterproof to protect the end-grain of the bamboo. The matching male has a spigot that is smaller in diameter than the shoulder section that fits over the rod, and a machined disc plugged into its tip; these three pieces are also soldered together. Such a ferrule is no less a work of craftsmanship than the rod it serves, and it deserves as much maintenance and attention.

THE INVENTION of the multipiece rod led in other directions as well, all the way up to today's fairly high-tech pack and travel rods. Makers of one-piece rods were limited in their choice of materials by whatever grew to the right length and shape, but this constraint went out the window when rod joints were developed. Now it was possible to use different materials for different sections of the rod–progressing from thicker, stouter woods at the butt to finer, more sensitive tips, depending on the demands of the water and the fish. A British outdoor writer of 1807 described a typical trout rod as being some 15 feet long and made of four materials: a seven-foot butt section of yellow deal, a six-foot length of hazel and then a "delicate piece of fine grained yew, exactly tapered, and ending in a point of whalebone, both making about two feet." The writer meant baleen fiber rather than true whalebone.

Equally important was that now certain rod woods could be hollowed out. One of the first reasons for doing this, as the "Treatise" suggested, was to carry the fine rod tip–by the 17th century tips were being made not only of baleen but even delicate tortoiseshell–out of harm's way, in a hollowed-out butt. (Gunsmiths had already figured out how to make long tubes, and Dame Juliana wrote in 1496 that a rod butt should be hollowed out with a hot wire.) Spare tips, or tips with different actions for different sorts of fishing, could be included as well. A few rod builders must have begun tinkering with naturally hollow woods too, perhaps trying shoots of bamboo in their multipiece rods.

Hollow sections are generally lighter sections, and they behave somewhat differently under flexing loads than do solid beams. The stress-strain relationships inherent in a hollow tube–where one wall is under tension and the other, opposite wall is being compressed when the tube is flexed–plague rod makers to this day. They search continually for new materials to let them make ever-lighter tapered tubes whose walls won't suddenly buckle under the tremendous flex of casting or fish-fighting.

Early rod makers couldn't quantify things like Modulus of Elasticity or hoop and beam strength, but they intuitively understood them and knew perfectly well what were desirable qualities, not only in fishing rods but in rod materials as well. They tried just about everything available in their search for the best combination of light weight, strength and delicacy. A partial list of domestic rod-making woods used in Europe and America includes ash, yew, fir, yellow deal and even chestnut and oak in the butts; and red deal, shadblow, Osage orange, hornbeam, elder, holly and hazel in mid- and upper sections. For today's collector, even specialists sometimes can't identify the woods used in a particular rod because all the sections were often stained or varnished to a uniform dark color.

The 18th and 19th centuries were the golden age of the British Empire. The Royal Navy and fleets of private explorers and entrepreneurs combed the globe for its treasures. The officers and leaders in particular were often sporting men, and they brought home exotic furs and feathers for tying their trout and salmon flies, and also rod-making woods that didn't grow at home in the United Kingdom. Some of the best were found in South America, the West Indies and nearby, in British Guyana, Jamaica and Cuba: washaba, which was strong and flexible but heavy and hard to cut; a close-grained exotic called blue mahoe, lighter and very resilient; and such stuff as bethabara, steelwood, snakewood and probably others. The two best, or at least most popular from this region, were greenheart and lancewood, and a few fly rods are still being made today of both these woods. (They are, in effect, instant collector's items–not to mention being quite pleasant and interesting to fish with.)

Greenheart is a giant of the laurel family. Its chief use apparently was in shipbuilding and the construction of piers and small bridges, for it is highly resistant to seawater. As a rod wood it's on the heavy side, but is so close-grained it can be cut to very fine diameters and tapers, and it is resilient and strong–if properly seasoned, finished against drying and then maintained. Greenheart is yellowy-brown, sometimes dark brown, and looks at first glance like cane, but of course the rod sections are round, not flat-sided. Lancewood is lighter in color and weight, not as strong, and often found its way into fly rod tips.

COLLECTORS of today generally focus on cane rods (as opposed to bamboo poles, which are single stalks of unworked bamboo), and American craftsmen come to the fore from that point on. According to some British tackle authorities, the chief contribution their former colony made to angling gear–before American split-cane rods and multiplying reels revolutionized the sport–was shipping hickory to England, where it was commonly used in the butts of less-expensive rods.

But that changed rapidly and decisively in the mid-1800s, thanks to Samuel and Solon Phillippe, father and son, gunsmiths of Pennsylvania. According to exhaustive research by tackle historian

Martin Keane, these two built the first known American split-cane rod sections, between about 1845 and 1860. These were of three- and four-strip construction (similar work had been done in Britain, and perhaps in America, 50 or more years earlier) and then, finally and significantly, in the six-strip style which would eventually dominate rod-making. The first known rod made entirely–each section, butt to tip–of six-strip cane was by Charles F. Murphy, of Newark, New Jersey, during the Civil War. He was a friend and admirer of the Phillippes, and went on, in Keane's words, to build "the first commercial split-bamboo rods in sufficient numbers to influence American anglers to use American-made rods." This was the beginning of the golden age of cane rods.

It is still astonishing to me that even the wand-like tip of a slender bamboo trout rod, maybe only a sixteenth of an inch thick, is made of six separate triangular strips glued together into a long, tapering, usually solid hexagon. Each fine strip is cut to included angles of sixty degrees–or a whisker less– so that their outside edges meet perfectly and there is room for the glue inside. Each strip also tapers precisely in thickness, to give the rod its final shape, strength and flex pattern.

When split bamboo became the rod material of choice, the hunt began for the best, most suitable of earth's thousand-odd species of bamboo. Calcutta cane, from India, held sway until the early 1900s, when Tonkin cane, with its high density of strong, resilient fibers, took over. Classified scientifically in 1931 as *Arundinaria amabilis* (loosely, "the lovely bamboo"), it grows only in the Guangdong Province of the People's Republic of China. For decades, tons and tons of it were imported by the New York firm of Harold Demarest. When the U.S. government slapped a trade embargo against newly Communist China shortly after World War II, rod companies thought they had enough stockpiled to see them through. The smaller shops did, and as they closed, one by one, the survivors snapped up the remaining cane. There is still pre-embargo bamboo out there, some of it more than 90 years old, well-seasoned by any standard. Large rod producers such as Orvis went to fantastic lengths, ranging from personal diplomacy to near smuggling, to try to keep the cane coming, while efforts to grow it elsewhere failed.

The Bamboo Curtain was breached in 1973, following the storied China tour of the U.S. ping-pong team, but the flow of high-quality, mature Tonkin cane has never been dependable. It arrives in New York Harbor in hundred-plus-pound bundles wrapped in burlap that is stencilled with exotic lettering. A straight, strong 12 foot culm, with no machete slashes or insect boreholes, makes a rod craftsman smile in anticipation, for it is a remarkable material. Metal-working tools must be used to shape it, and a machinist's file that's become too dull to cut cane will still file ordinary carbon steel.

The initial inspection may junk half or more of a shipment of bamboo. It is, after all, a natural material, with all the imperfections to be expected from good and bad growth years, insects, disease and imperfect harvesting or seasoning. Select raw culms–often flame- or oven-tempered, which imparts a lovely honey-brown tone–are split apart: The maker bravely taps a small froe into the end of a culm. Like good stovewood, it cracks apart again and again; the grain determines the splits, and the rod maker only initiates them. (Rod crafters who cut their rough strips with table saws sometimes junk three-quarters of them because the saw teeth can rip through the valuable long fibers of the culm instead of separating them.) The rings on the outside of the cane are nodes, divisions between the cells of the stalk. The membrane inside is cut away, and the bumps outside are filed down. Particularly thick walled strips may be fed through a power planer to mill away the useless inner pith. The strong fibers are near the outside edge.

The next step is to shape the sticks. Many one-man rod shops still lay them into metal forms of exact depth and shape, and plane off the excess that protrudes above the slot. Naturally, every rod model requires a different set of forms. A few makers have bevelers, machines that cut a precise, tapered triangular segment out of each stick. When Hiram Leonard invented the power beveler, around 1876, it turned the rod business around, for suddenly it became possible to manufacture dozens of identical segments in what seemed almost no time, and to within repeatable tolerances of a few thousandths of an inch. (It is no less incredible that bamboo, a plant, subject to the whims of its environment, can tread so fine a line.)

Leonard was well aware of what he had wrought. His production beveler was installed in a special locked room at the factory, in Bangor, Maine, and even trusted employees were threatened with instant dismissal should they enter. But word got out, inevitably, and other bevelers appeared. The history of one of them is worth following, for it illustrates how past and present are woven together in this cottage industry:

Today, master rod builder Walt Carpenter uses a beveler that was made in 1890 for Fred E. Thomas, Eustis Edwards and Loman Hawes. They were H.L. Leonard Company people who went into partnership for themselves after Leonard moved to Central Valley, New York. In its early years the machine made the now-classic Kosmic rods sold by A.G. Spaulding in New York City.

When Hawes died in 1891, a young man named Edward Payne came aboard, and the company moved out of the Catskill Mountains to Brooklyn. F.E. Thomas, however, quit and went to Brewer, Maine, where he installed a commercial laundry in the basement below his own rod shop. (Cane-rod makers have rarely prospered financially.) In 1898 Kosmic production stopped; Eustis Edwards took off and traveled the West as a photographer while Ed Payne moved the beveler out to Highland Mills, New York, and set up the renowned E.F. Payne Rod Manufactory.

The machine then was shipped to Brewer in the mid-'20s when Payne sold it back to Thomas and Edwards, who had returned from his adventures and rejoined his friend in Maine. The two then relocated a few miles down the Penobscot River, in Bangor, where the beveler stayed until their F.E. Thomas Company went out of business in 1958. A rod maker named Sam (Clarence H.) Carlson brought the beveler to Hampden, Connecticut, where he made his own famous four-sided "quadrate" rods. Carlson sold the beveler in 1973 to Walt Carpenter—who was the last rod maker employed at Payne when that firm went out of business in 1978. (Jim Payne, son of Edward and a "master's master" rod maker, had died in 1968.) That year Carpenter went into business for himself and moved to Chester, New York, finally bringing the Thomas beveler full circle. Now it's cutting cane only a few miles from where it began a century ago. Everyone connected with it has earned a spot in the pantheon of collectable rod makers.

To return to rod construction: From the resultant pile of cane segments, six good ones—no splinters, cracks, other defects—must be "mis-matched" properly together, making sure no two nodes lie next to each other to produce a weak spot. The inner surfaces of the segments are liberally painted with a hide glue, which flows better than epoxy and remains slightly plastic when cured. The only drawback to such a glue is its water-solubility, potentially fatal in a fishing rod. Some rods are varnished for waterproofing, some are impregnated with an acrylic or other resin compound, which produces a near-perfect finish that can be rejuvenated, even years later, simply by buffing. Impregnation finishes were developed in the 1940s (by Wes Jordan, the celebrated designer, craftsman and production engineer who put Orvis in the forefront of the rod business) but the process is still regarded with suspicion in some anglers' and collectors' circles. Done properly, it does *not* produce a "soggy" rod.

The glued-up rod blank is then wrapped back and forth with string, to keep all in position. Dry, the string is unraveled and the excess glue and any rough spots are scraped and sanded off. This is the moment of truth. If the blank doesn't flex properly, if it has a pronounced stiff spine along one axis, there's no point in continuing with the trimming, straightening, ferruling and furnishing with grip, reel seat, line guides and other fittings. If all goes well, about one month may have passed by the time the rod is shipped, and many top rod makers are a year or more back-ordered.

Like the best wrist watches, reels, guns and automobiles, such a rod represents many hours of one man's life and is the sum to date of his years of experience as both angler and craftsman. There is value here, and the demand is understandable.

THERE is a tendency now, at least among the uninitiated, to regard any and all "old" (e.g., unearthed in Grandad's attic) split-bamboo rods as valuable antiques. As family mementos or handsome examples of craftsmanship, they may be worth keeping or collecting; they may even be fairly old. Few, unfortunately, are valuable—yet. The split-cane rod made today is a rare, limited-production, labor-intensive item for which the maker charges anywhere from $350 to about $3,000; it is by nature a high-class item. However, throughout much of this century, until fiberglass took over the market in the 1950s, most fishing rods were routinely made of cane, Calcutta or Tonkin. (Between the world wars came a few oddities such as steel fishing rods. For example, the telescoping True Temper, Bristol and other models that are beginning to attract attention from collectors.) Truly top-grade cane rods were as rare and, comparatively, as expensive then as now; it's just that the middle and lower levels of the rod market were also occupied by cane. Thanks to Hiram Leonard's beveler, many American companies—Montague, Cross, Chubb, Heddon, Phillipson, Uslan, Granger, Wright & McGill, South Bend, Pelham, Frost, Bristol, Dunton, Devine, Shakespeare among them—were able to mass-produce thousands and thousands of split-cane fly rods, bait rods, casting rods, boat rods, surf rods and even heavy-duty trolling and big-game rods, for every hardware store and sporting-goods outlet in America. Naturally, there were also many private-label cane rods made for companies ranging from Abercrombie & Fitch to Sears, Roebuck and Montgomery Ward; some are of estimable quality. (For example, L.L. Bean's "99" rods were made by The Orvis Company.) The technology of splitting, tapering and gluing together strips of bamboo into immensely strong and flexible shafts was so much a part of the American scene that items as diverse as violin bows and ski poles, golf clubs and net handles were made that way. There was nothing rare about split bamboo, but the rods of the masters were and remain vastly different from ordinary fishing rods.

Having thrown out this *caveat*, let me backtrack to my first remark, at the top of the previous paragraph: Many tackle connoisseurs regard *any* cane rod as superior to any rod made of synthetics. Everyone can appreciate the warm glow, the organic feel, the aura of hand-craftsmanship that a split-cane rod gives off, and the pride and pleasure of ownership. So let's be thankful that so many were turned out in that century before fiberglass, for without these still-inexpensive old cane rods—on tables at any flea market—the beginning rod collector would be left high and dry, frustrated by the spiralling prices of those few rods made by the masters. The better grades of the mass-market rods are beginning to appreciate now also, and it is safe to say that as time takes its toll of this large-but-limited pool of rods, values will keep on escalating.

COMPARED to cane, fiberglass rods could be refreshingly light and strong, as well as resistant to fatigue, the elements, and neglect. Tackle manufacturers appreciated the ease with which they could be churned out inexpensively, which was important as labor costs spiralled upward and the sportfishing market boomed in postwar America. While cane required a knowing hand and eye to work, was always in short supply and often varied drastically in quality from shipment to shipment, fiberglass was a push-button synthetic. Using it, the human and natural factors could be largely removed. Rod manufacturers had to go through a period of experimentation and learning before settling on hollow-tube construction, but a few of the old solid-blanks are still around. At the moment, they have little value except as curios.

Fishing rods of "ACM"—Advanced Composite Materials, namely graphite and boron—appeared on tackle shop racks in the early 1970s, and touched off another storm of controversy. Purists reckoned that the final blow had been struck against rods, that the trend toward totally automated production that had begun with glass was now complete. In the glass era, detractors spread stories of surf casters disemboweled when their heavy rod snapped under load and drove the jagged end back through their waders and clothing. Some who hated graphite claimed that when these latest "monstrosities" shattered they fired a swarm of toxic graphite splinters into the angler's skin, where no X-ray machine would be able to find them. The fuss and the apocryphal stories died down rapidly when manufacturers debugged their processes and their products. Possibly the same kind of stories circulated when Hiram Leonard began "mass-producing" cane rods on his beveling machine.

As with most types of fiberglass, a graphite rod blank is molded on a steel mandrel precisely tapered to produce a fishing rod of a particular length, weight, action and "feel." The input of a skilled human designer is as critical now as it ever was; the difference is that when the prototyping is complete, identical rods can theoretically be produced in vast quantities by people who have no idea how a fishing rod should perform. But craftsmanship is still needed when the blanks are popped off their mandrels after oven-curing. Butts and tips have to be matched up; ferrules, reel seats, grips, line guides and windings have to be added; and all by hand. In large part, only the rod material is different—it grows in an evacuated labratory oven instead of on a remote Chinese hillside.

The end product is simply the best fishing tool ever made. No other fishing rod is so strong yet so light, flexible and vibration-free. In fly-fishing, where rod action is especially important, graphite has added 15 or 20 feet to the distance the average angler can cast. But collectors and purists spurn the unfortunate fiber rod. It is an unlovely thing and it excites no emotional response; like a quartz wrist watch, it merely does its job extremely well.

Whether today's graphite rod ever becomes tomorrow's collectible seems a bit doubtful. Graphite and epoxy are highly inert materials, so these rods won't simply molder away like wood or cane that has been forgotten. Most are expensive enough that few of us will ever throw one away or use it as a tomato stake when it's become obsolete or when we take up radio-control aircraft instead. And they rarely break. As rods from the 1970s and '80s become old, they'll be with us in large numbers for a long time. The outlook for collectors seeking spiralling values is not promising.

There are some exceptions. Most of the designers who pioneered and are now perfecting these composite rods are still alive today; many are still, in 1989, in the tackle business. In their offices and workshops and rod closets at home are stacked prototypes, samples and pre-production glass and graphite rods made by their own hands, and these may be tomorrow's highly desirable collectibles. Many of these rods are unsigned, unnumbered, and are identified in no catalogs or magazine articles. Provenance will be critically important. But, as I say, their creators are still with us, still able to identify these rods and set the record straight . . . .

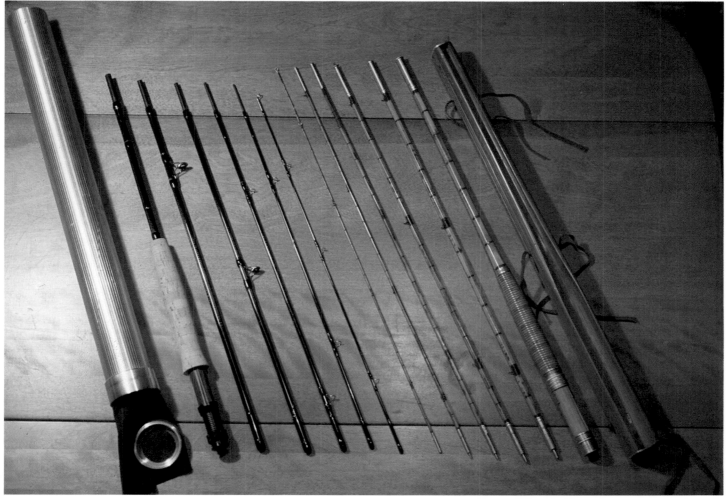

THIS SIX-PIECE split-bamboo fly rod was built by John Krider, of Philadelphia, around 1900. Assembled, it is ten feet long. Note the nickel-silver pin ferrules, the loose ring-type line guides, the finely knurled plugs in the female ferrules, and the fitted wooden rod holder. The Krider, though it is of six-strip construction, is slimmer and more delicate than the modern hollow graphite travel rod next to it. Photograph by Dick Finlay.

Son
e'' four-strip bamboo/7 feet/3 ounces

John Krider (Philadelphia)
circa 1885/six-piece "valise" rod/10

A Museum purchase

THE SAME six-piece split-bamboo "valise" rod built by John Krider, on display at The American Museum of Fly Fishing, in Manchester, Vermont. The rod above it is a W.E. Edwards & Sons fly rod of "quadrate," or four-strip cane construction, made in about 1950. Photograph courtesy of The American Museum of Fly Fishing.

A TEN-FOOT, four-piece pack rod, in its wooden valise case with string ties; note the many extra sections provided with the rod. The reel is a Kosmic raised-pillar multiplier (serial #936). Photograph courtesy of The American Museum of Fly Fishing.

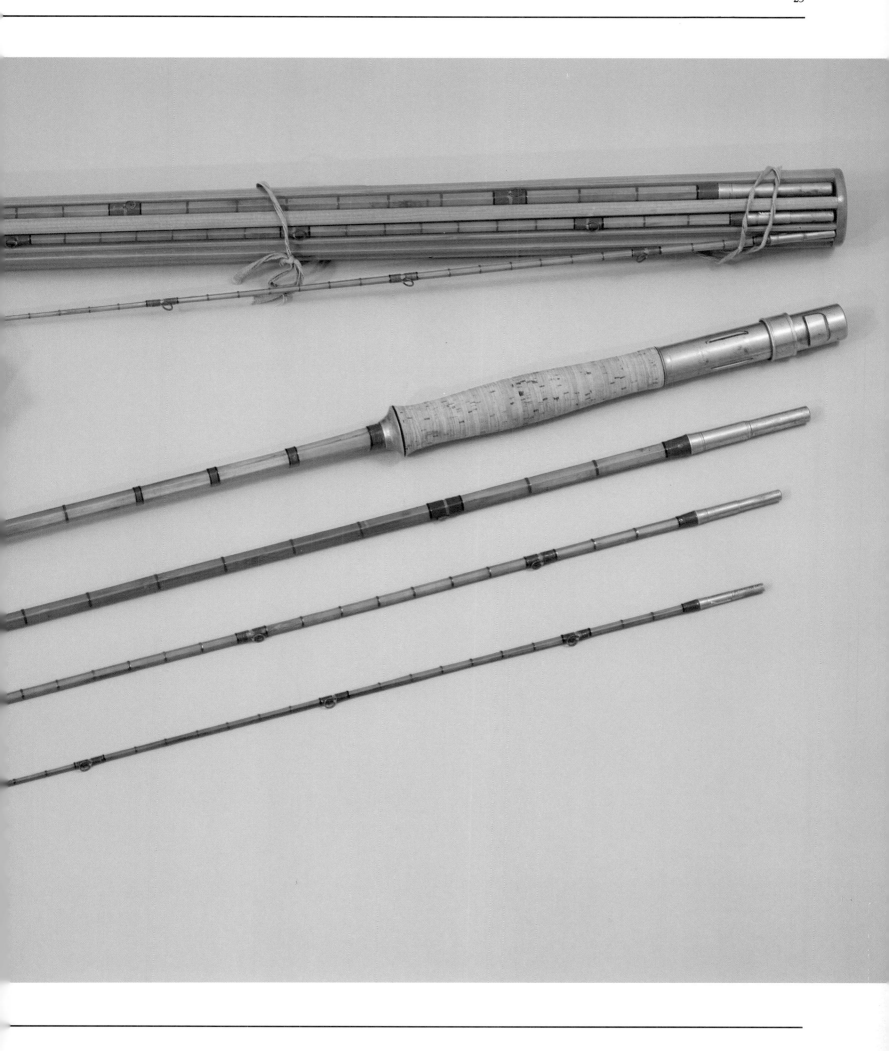

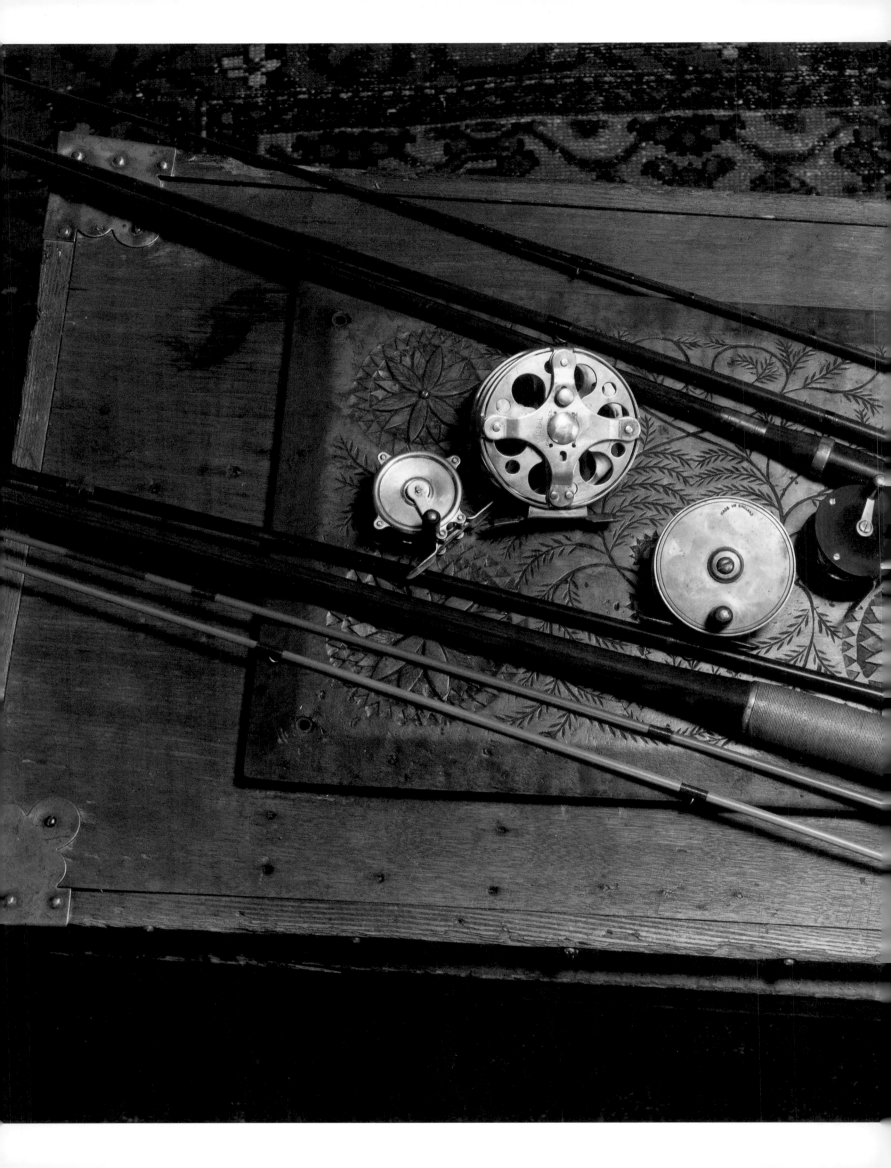

EARLY AMERICAN solid-wood rods. The foreground rod, which dates from the 1850s, has a greenheart butt and midsection and tips made of lemonwood. Note also the spike ferrules and the wound rattan grip. The other rod is all greenheart; it is inscribed with the single word "Philadelphia." The open-frame reel is an "Ideal," perhaps made by Meisselbach. The raised-pillar reel is an inexpensive stamped imitation of a Leonard. Photograph by Michael L. Melo.

A FOUR-PIECE, *twelve-foot rod of solid ash, built in New York in 1847 by the B.D. Welch tackle company, who presented it to the great statesman Daniel Webster. The rod was restored by the Smithsonian Institute; its tip has not survived. The inscription reads "Daniel Webster, Marshfield, Mass." Photograph courtesy of The American Museum of Fly Fishing.*

Daniel Webster
Marshfield
Mass.

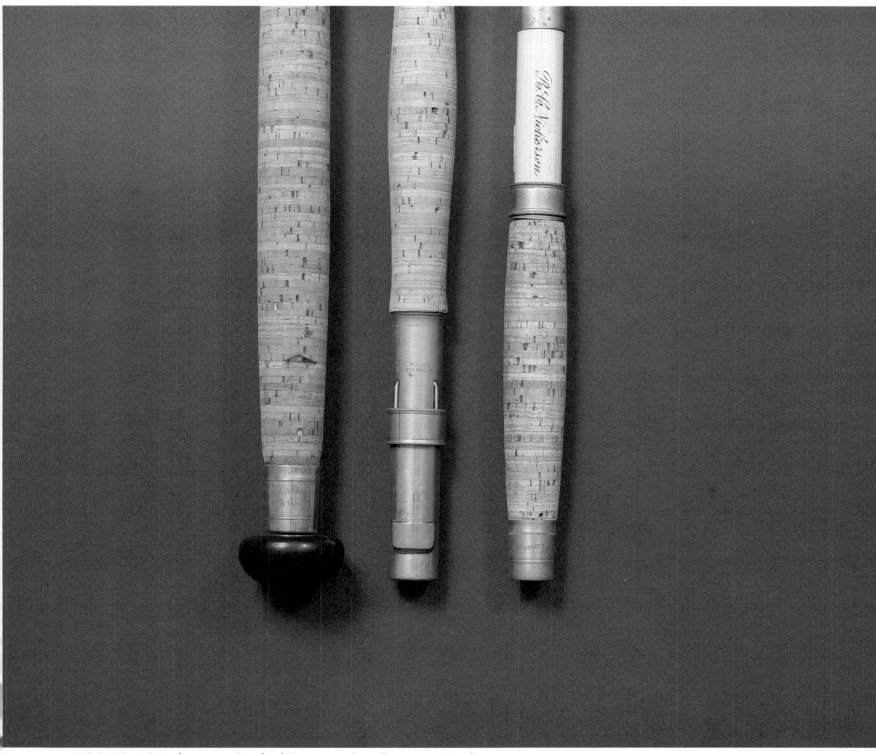

KOSMIC ROD close-ups. On the left is a 14-foot three-piece "Isaak Walton" salmon rod built after the U.S. Net & Twine Co. bought out Thomas, Edwards & Payne. At center is a ten-foot, four-piece pack rod. The third is a three-piece 8-foot, 4-inch bass rod that belonged to a Mr. R.C. Nickerson. All three grips show the very thin cork rings that were used around the turn of the 20th Century. Photograph courtesy of The American Museum of Fly Fishing.

A RATHER battered 8 1/2-foot three-piece bamboo trout fly rod made by E.C. Powell. Its collectibility stems from the owner's name penned above the grip: naturalist Aldo Leopold. The flies and fly-tying tools and materials were the property of Capt. Mark Kerridge, a California angling collector and historian, and the wicker-and-leather creel reputedly belonged to Gen. George S. Patton, Jr. Don Gray Photograph courtesy of The American Museum of Fly Fishing.

30

A PAIR of H.L. Leonard fly rods. Below is a three-piece 8 1/2-foot "honey-wrap" rod, probably made in the 1920s, long after the company left Bangor, Maine. The red-wrap nine-foot rod dates from about World War I; it belonged to sporting artist Milton Weiler. The William Mills company, of New York City, was an active dealer in Leonard tackle. The raised-pillar reel on the left is also a Leonard; at center is an unusual shiny-sideplate Julius Vom Hofe trout reel. The gut-snelled flies and British hand vise date from the same period. Photograph by Michael L. Melo.

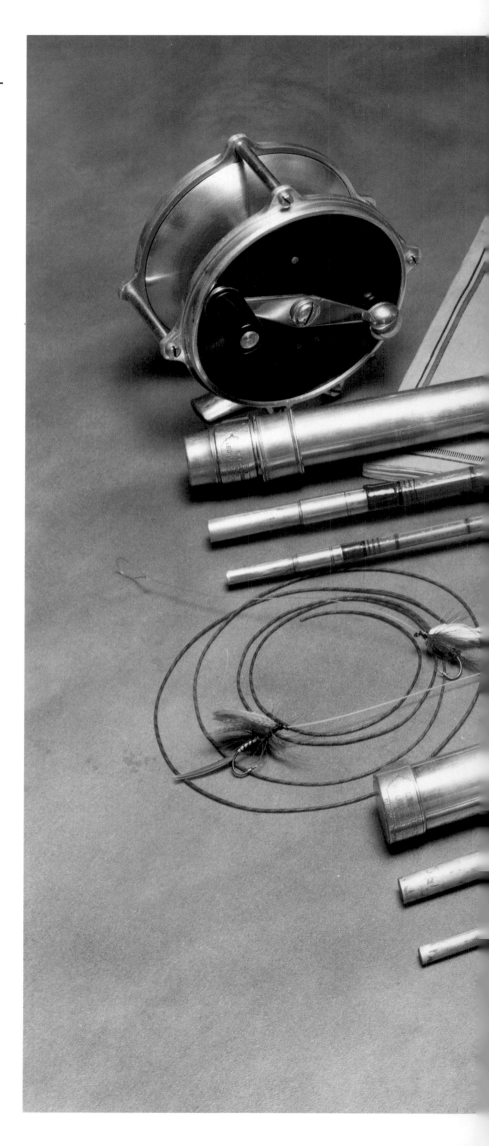

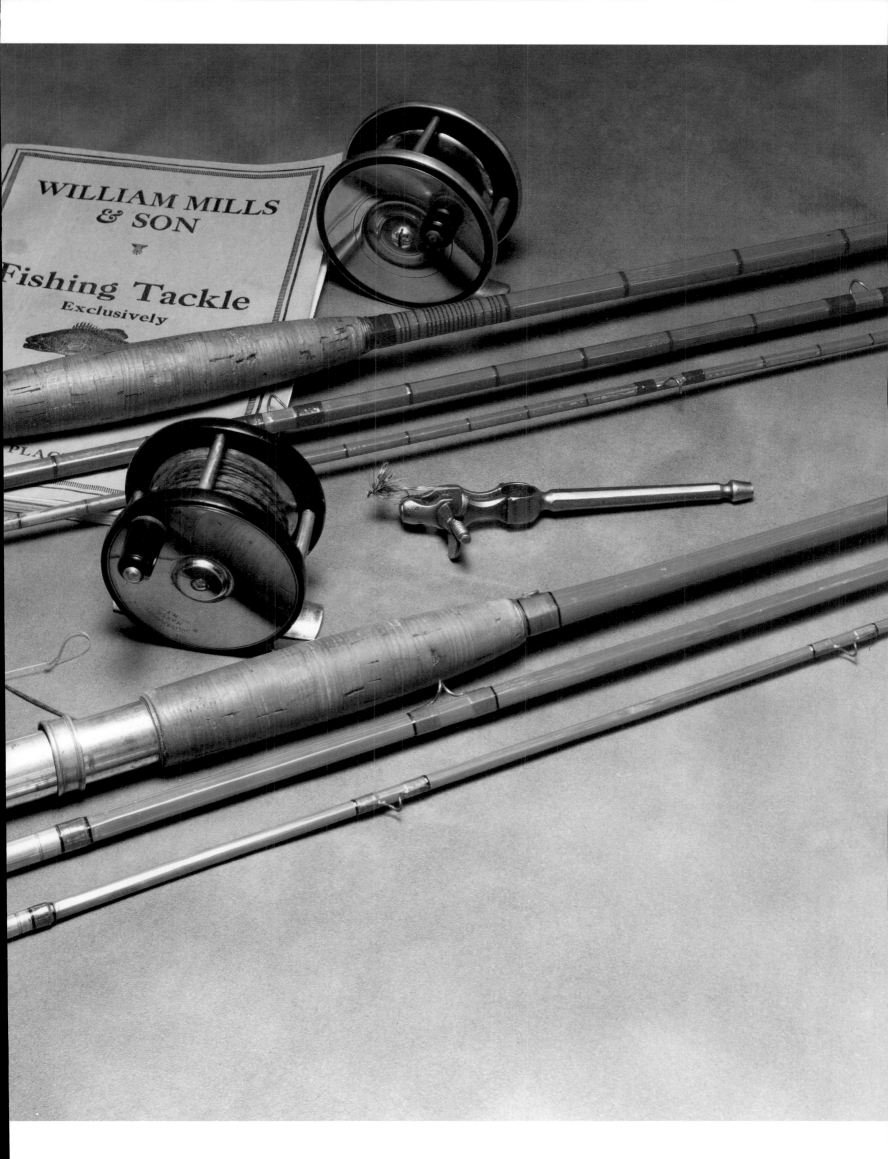

THE FLY rod on the left is an eight-foot three-piece F.E. Thomas, its two tips protected by an unusual screw-top bamboo tube. The other rod is a 7 1/2-foot Goodwin Granger. The reel between them is a pre-WWII Hardy Uniqua, and the backdrop is a book of Currier & Ives angling prints. The reels at the back are, left, a Meisselbach "Catucci" and a Julius Vom Hofe. Photograph by Michael L. Melo.

TOP ROW, left to right: two H.L. Leonard rods—a nine-footer and an eight-footer, with full metal reel seats—and a seven-foot F.E. Thomas; an eight-foot Hardy, and an 8 1/2-foot Millwards, with brass spike ferrules. Bottom: eight-foot and nine-foot Garrisons, with their distinctive grips and reel seats; and an eight-foot F.E. Thomas. The oldest rods are the three on the upper left, which date back to about 1920 (note the intermediate thread wraps on the Thomas). The reels include, at bottom, a Hardy "St. George," a Vom Hofe, at right, and a raised-pillar Leonard. Photograph by Michael L. Melo.

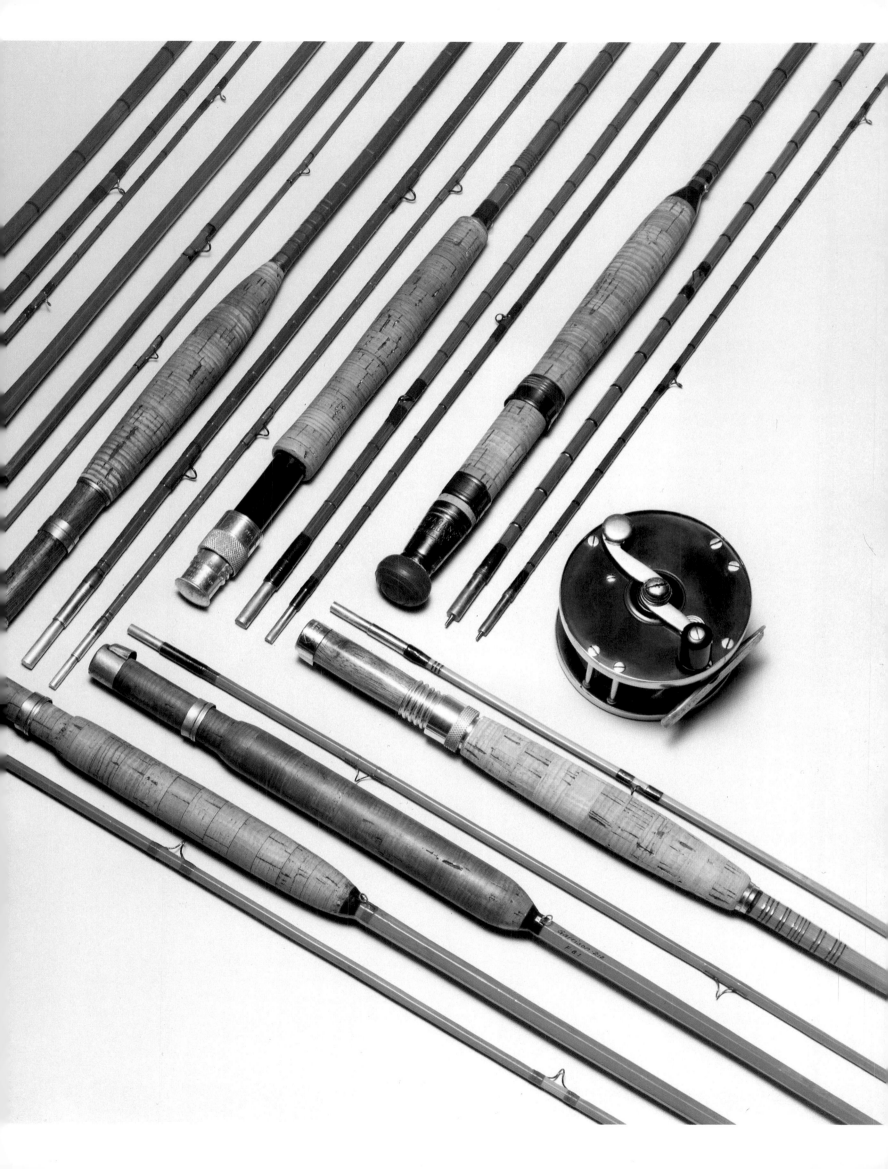

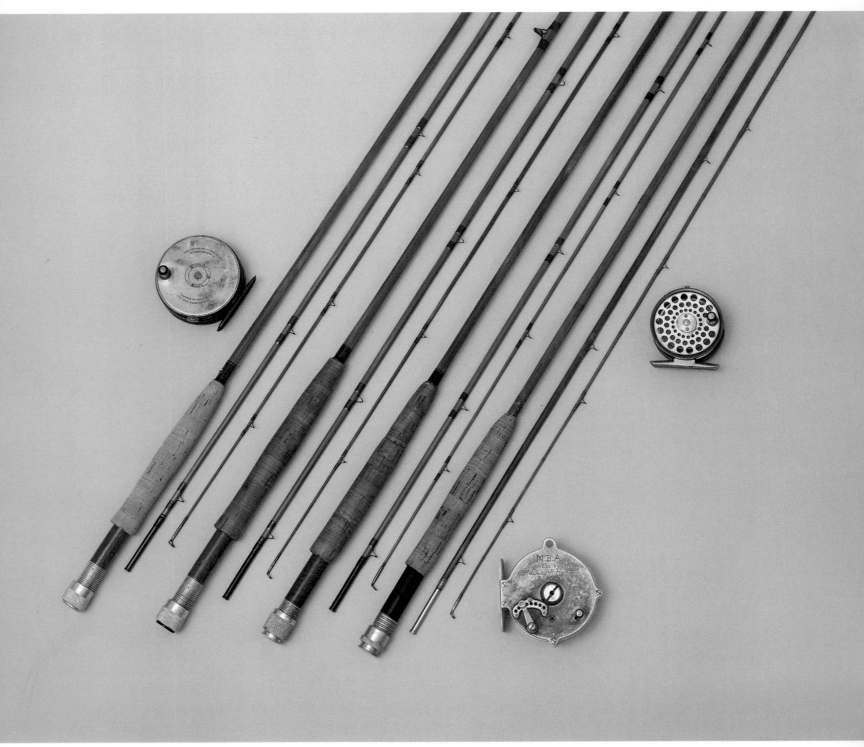

FLY RODS built by master craftsman Jim Payne, who took over the E.F. Payne Rod Company, in Highland Mills, New York, in 1914, when his famous father, Edward, passed away. By the time he died, in 1968, Jim had made thousands of highly regarded split-cane rods and was regarded as the most important rod builder of the modern era.

The reels are, left to right, a Hardy Bros. LRH "Lightweight" originally sold by Abercrombie & Fitch in New York; a raised-pillar trout reel made and probably used by Edward R. Hewitt, author of "A Trout and Salmon Fisherman for Seventy-Five Years," among other works; and an early Hardy "Princess." Photograph courtesy of The American Musuem of Fly Fishing.

THOMAS CHUBB was a major American tackle manufacturer in the 1880s and '90s, located in Post Mills, Vermont. The company was absorbed by the Montague Rod Company, of Massachusetts, shortly after the turn of the century. This rod dates from about 1885.

MODERN NICKEL-SILVER ferrules and reel-seat sliding band and cap, specially engraved to enhance their value as part of an investment-grade bamboo rod—in this case, one of the "Amabilis" series of split-cane fly rods, limited to 20, made by the Thomas & Thomas Rod Company in 1985.

MODERN STRAIGHT-GRIP split-cane baitcasting rods made by Thomas & Thomas, in 5 1/2 and 6-foot lengths, two-piece style, for quarter-ounce and 3/8-ounce lures. The antique reels are a Coxe (left) and a Meek Bluegrass tournament reel.

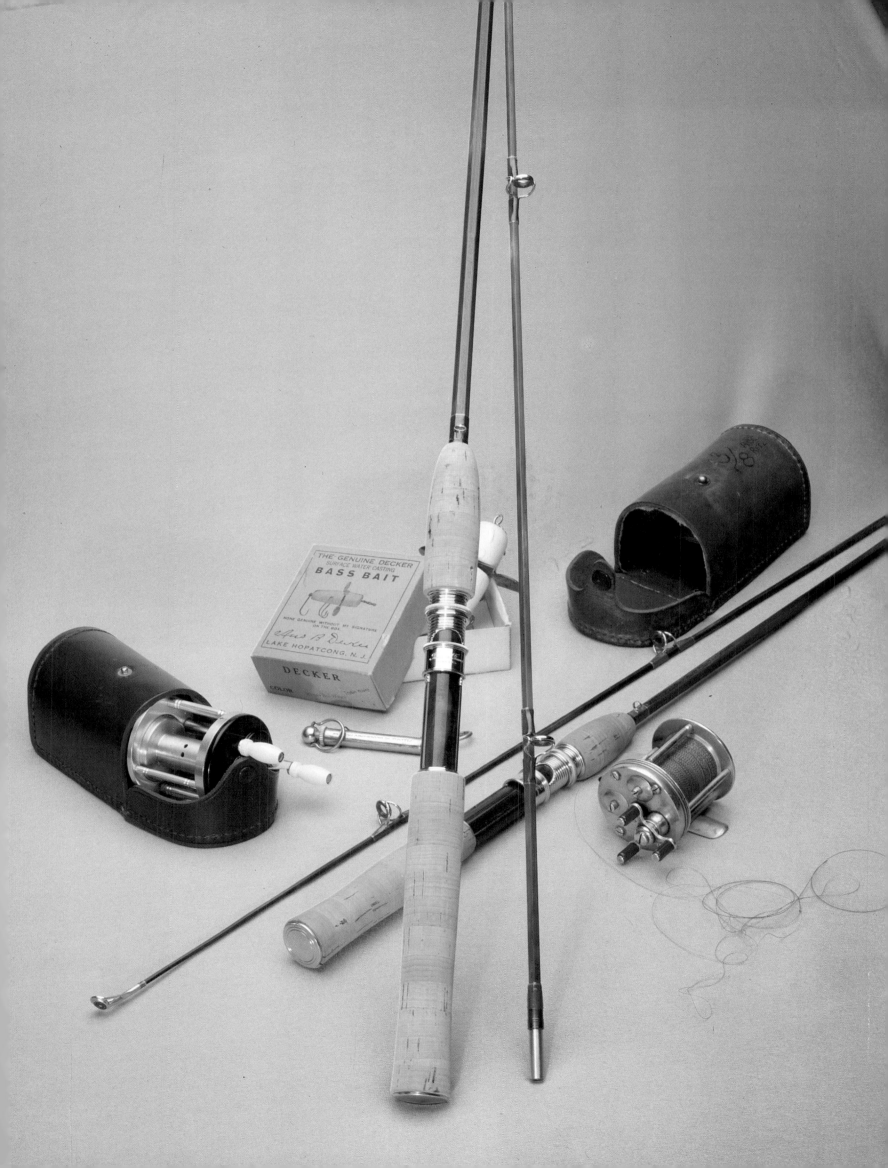

DON'T BOTHER looking for this rod at flea markets. Made by Thomas & Thomas, of Turners Falls, Massachusetts, it was commissioned in 1982 by President Ronald Reagan as a gift for Malcolm Fraser, Prime Minister of Australia. Note the presidential seal, the ferrule plugs, and the detachable fighting butt. Mr. Fraser is a keen angler, to the point that, on a later visit to the U.S., he drove to Turners Falls to fish with Tom Dorsey, T&T's chief rod maker.

EIGHT OF the most desirable contemporary bamboo fly rods, all made by Thomas & Thomas. Clockwise, beginning with the cased rod: T&T's 10th Anniversary rod, 1979—a series of 10 eight-foot two-piece rods, for five-weight lines, with Spanish mahogany spliced into the bamboo segments to form the swelled butt • A "Sans Noeud" 7 1/2-foot two-piece five-weight rod (from a series of 20 made in 1981); the nodes were cut out of the cane and the rod segments were spliced together in long, overlapping "darts" • The 1983 "Fountainhead" (lying down), with its distinctive spike ferrules and extra-long wooden grip and reel seat, was built to commemorate the first American split-cane craftsmen, Phillippe, Mitchell, Murphy, and Greene; it too has Spanish mahogany spliced into the swelled butt • A "one of one" unissued 7 1/2-foot three-piece nodeless-construction rod, for four-weight lines, built in 1982 • One of 15 "Catskill Legend" rods, a series of three-piece eight-footers made to help the Catskill Fly Fishing Museum raise funds; the names of 13 famous Catskills anglers, from Theodore Gordon to Harry Darbee and Art Flick, are engraved on the full nickel-silver reel seat • Leaning against its leather tube is a 1985 "Amabilis" rod, another of an edition limited to 20, which pays homage to the bamboo—Arundinaria amabilis—from which these rods are crafted and whose fully engraved ferrules and fittings appear elsewhere in this book • The rod with the "Ivoroid" reel seat and the red intermediate wraps is T&T's "Kosmic Commemorative," issued in 1984; the original rod had a celluloid reel seat, not ivory, and this one is actually micarta, as celluloid is now a controlled substance • Another "one of one" unissued rod, built in 1980, with a rosewood swelled-splice butt and alternating bands of cork and rosewood in the grip (note that wood and cane are both visible below the reel seat hood). The raised-pillar reel is also a Kosmic Commemorative, commissioned by Thomas & Thomas.

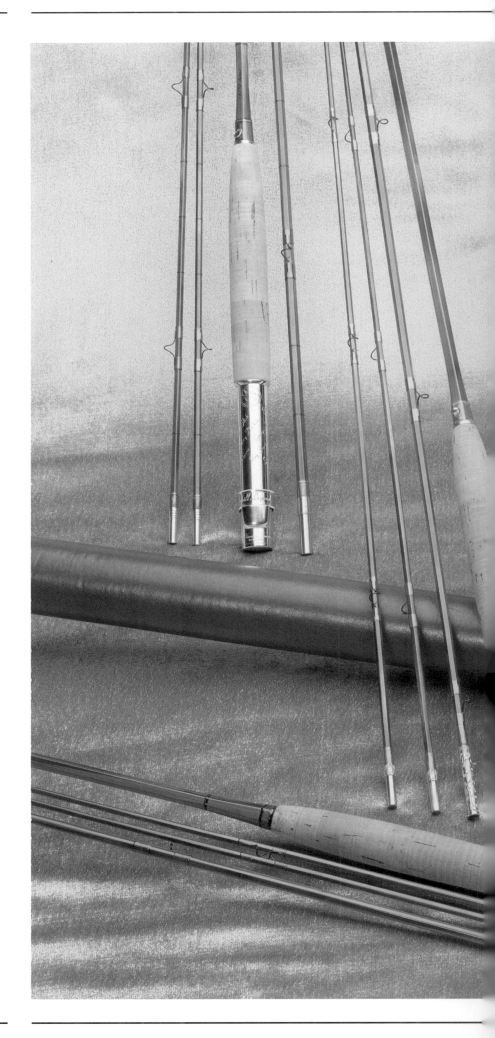

MASTER ROD builder Walt Carpenter, of Chester, New York, is one of those artisans who make fine split-bamboo rods in a style that has hardly changed in a century. The criteria for judging such a modern cane rod are the same used to evaluate an antique. Are the glue seams nearly invisible? Is the flame-coloring even throughout? Does the rod blank twist to one side or another? And the furnishings—are the knurlings and stampings on the metalwork bright and sharp-edged? The ferrules—are they securely mounted and fitted together so they don't click? Were any burrs left behind? Do the line guides sit up straight and proper? Are the thread windings tight and clean, proportionately spaced and trimmed? Overall, is the rod's finish deep and lustrous, free of dust or bubbles? Is the flex crisp, clean, vigorous?

AN ENTIRE culm of precious pre-Chinese-embargo Tonkin bamboo passes through the flame for coloring and tempering. When repairing old rods, Carpenter burns Pentane, an obsolete fuel, to get a perfect match between old and new bamboo. That's Jim Payne's apron he's wearing.

WITH FROE and then hammer and chisel, Walt splits the culm into rough strips. Some rod builders use a table saw to rip the bamboo; Walt prefers to let the natural grain determine the split.

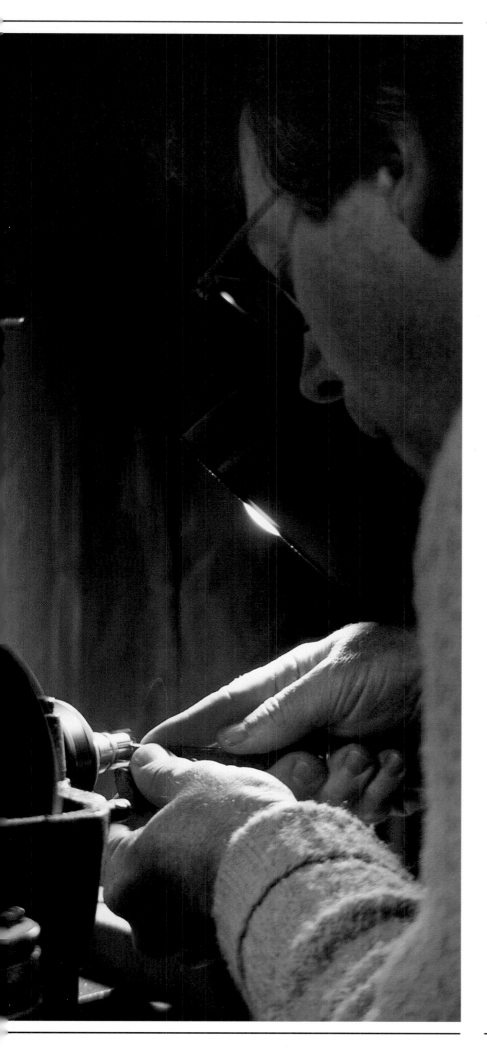

THE STRIPS then pass through the famous Thomas beveler, which cuts them to a triangular cross-section and also tapers them, butt to tip. Note the twin saw heads, set at just over 60 degrees apart.

TURNING A nickel-silver rod butt cap on a lathe.

SIX TRIANGULAR-SECTION strips are then carefully "mis-matched" together and glued into one hexagonal-section rod segment. Here, after the glue has dried and the blank been sanded, Walt painstakingly fits a nickel-silver ferrule. When butt and tip sections go together for the first time, and Walt flexes the whole rod blank, he'll know whether two weeks' work and a stick of cane have been wasted or not.

THE FINISHED product. The smaller rod is a new carpenter trout rod; the other is a heavy, two-handed antique salmon rod that Walt has repaired. The reel is a Bogdan.

REELS

ANGLERS know, and collectors should know, that there are at least three ways of looking at a fishing reel: as a storage depot, a casting device, and/or a fish-fighting tool. A fly reel, for example, is often just a convenient place to keep unused line out of the way but accessible. A spinning or baitcasting reel, on the other hand, is designed to help send the hook out over the water. And a big-game trolling reel falls into the last category—its primary function is to brake the near-unstoppable surges of a great sea fish. All but the most elemental reels, however, combine two or even all three of these functions: Since before Zane Grey's day as a pioneer in offshore fishing, big-game reels have served as line-storage "drums" as well as fighting-drag machines. Most trout-size fly reels and virtually all larger models also perform exactly the same functions—provide room for enough line to conquer the intended trophy, plus some form of spool brake, be it internal/mechanical or external and applied by hand. Technologically the most sophisticated fishing reels, today and a century ago, are those that offer all three functions: storage (easy—just make the spool large enough), drag (some adjustable way to apply friction), and castability. That means letting line peel or unroll off the storage spool so easily that it helps, or at least doesn't hinder, the cast. Often these reels also have some kind of spool-overrun brake, to reduce backlash while casting; even with such a brake, they can be the most demanding to learn to use.

Fly fishermen and trollers pull line off the reel before they cast or otherwise put their lures to work. Baitcasters and spinfishermen work directly off their reels. These differences are woven deeply into the centuries-old distinctions between methods of sportfishing—which may help determine who gets into which clubs.

From the collector's viewpoint, reels may be the most interesting of all tackle. They exist in a tremendous variety of sizes, shapes, intended uses, and mechanical complexity. They are often beautifully made and beautiful to look at. Finally, and most important, they *do* something. Unlike a rod or a lure, a fishing reel spins and clicks and purrs in the hand. Reel collectors keep their trophies on shelves under glass, but they always have one or two on their desks where they can fondle them like worry beads.

AS WITH fishing rods, the very earliest and simplest type of reel is still in wide use today. We have cane-pole and hand–line fishermen. It doesn't take a degree in mechanical engineering to "invent" a stick around which to wind surplus line. Sophistication began to creep in when the fisherman–an ancient Egyptian or Athapascan, let's say–carved a length of wood, ivory or bone with special pins or horns on each end to hold the line neatly in place. This innovation increased the line-holding capacity of the stick *and* the speed with which the line could be deployed or taken up. Very important, for although these are still only storage devices and not put into play during the actual fishing, their developers were already on the path that led eventually–by way of the Nottingham "wynche" and the Kentucky multiplier–to today's adjustable-drag, magnetically controlled, digital-readout, level-wind baitcasting reel.

There were quite a few interesting, if not outright odd, stops along the route, particularly in England. In the 18th and early 19th centuries, British fishermen might use belly pirns–large wooden winches that were worn on the waist, mounted on stout leather belts rather than on the rod. Or they might favor the bank runner, which was a free-turning spool of line mounted vertically atop a spike; the fisherman drove the spike into the stream bank, baited and cast out the hook and float, and retired to the shade of a tree to wait for action. There were even water borne versions of the bank runner, known as men-o-war or kill-devils. These were wide grooved spools, made to float vertically on a lake while the hook hung in the water beneath. When a fish took the bait, the line slipped out of its notch on the spool rim and uncoiled easily as the fish swallowed the morsel. When the line paid out completely, things began to happen, and there are many accounts of the "great fun" when a dozen or more kill-devils were plowing in different directions across some Scottish lake.

American Indians are said to have used hollow gourds in the same way, and today in the lower Mississippi Valley fishermen "jug" for giant catfish with drifting plastic bottles. The resemblance is more to a bobber than to a fishing reel, however.

No European fisherman or gunsmith gets the credit for inventing the fishing reel; to judge by the various known 17th century treatises, reels–or "winds," as they were called–were already then a fact of life, apparently evolving slowly along with rods and every other part of fishing tackle. Moreover, there is a celebrated painting by the Chinese artist Ma Yuan, of the Sung Dynasty (960-1280 A.D.), that shows a boat fisherman with what is unmistakably a reel attached to his rod. Angling authority A.J. McClane writes that although the painting was known in art circles, it had never been brought to the attention of the fishing world until Dr. John T. Bonner, of Princeton University, published it in *The Atlantic Salmon Journal* in 1967. Thus, fishing reels join gunpowder, pasta, the compass and so on on the long list of "modern" inventions that the ancient Chinese developed well ahead of the West. John Orrelle, in his excellent *Fly Reels of the Past*, cites other evidence that may push the invention of the fishing reel in China back as far as 300 A.D. He emphasizes that reels were logically more likely to develop in cultures that used the wheel, the windlass and the bobbin (in fabric arts), and of course the ancient Chinese—ancient by Western standards, that is—were masters of all three technologies.

In the 1600s, English winches, or winds, were made almost entirely of wood—walnut or oak, and then, as industry began to import them in quantity, mahogany and rosewood. Some, home-made perhaps, featured spools that were crude barrel shapes held inside cut-out frames that were lashed or pinned to the rod butt. Others, especially into the 18th century, also wood, were obviously luxury items for the well-to-do sportsman, made with the same craftsmanship and attention to detail that characterizes the furniture of that era. These had the deeply dished, pulley-wheel type spools we associate today with fly reels. Wooden machine parts wore out quickly, however, and reel evolution progressed with iron and brass spindles, pillars (the crossbars that separate the frame plates), cranks, feet, and check and drag mechanisms. By the 1770s the big news was the multiplying reel, where one turn of the crank handle produced three or four revolutions of the spool, for faster line take-up. As machinists worked out multiple gear trains and tooth counts, multiplier ratios of up to nine-to-one eventually appeared, but these were not very practical. The resultant high speed of the spool decreased the fisherman's mechanical winching advantage and "feel," and could wear out even metal parts and bearings quickly. Early multipliers, moreover, were not anti-reverse types—the handles turned backwards when the fish took line out, and, thanks to the gearing, at a rate that could bruise or even break fingers.

(Multiplying reels were somewhat controversial in the late 1700s; some writers of that era dismissed them as unreliable gadgets. Interestingly enough, two centuries later, we still hear multiplying fly reels, of virtually the same design but with rust-proof and low-wear gears and bushings, dismissed as "too delicate" and "trouble-prone." But quite a few companies keep on making them, and evidently quite a few fishermen keep on buying and, presumably, using them. Modern spinning and baitcasting reels, of course, all employ a gear drive for higher spool speeds. Fly fishermen have always been more conservative.)

The multiplying reel became much more popular in America, and went on to reach its peak here, while English fishermen stayed with their "centre-pin" reel, the wooden-spool Nottingham type. (Nottingham is in the English Midlands, where the reel originated.) So many were made, well into this century, that they are now a staple at present-day tackle auctions and swap meets, and they've launched many reel collectors upon the true path. Nottinghams, with their brass or even silver fittings and their double crank handles, are big, bulky and heavy, but undeniably handsome. The wooden spool generally turns on a brass or iron spindle and is often held in place against its wooden back plate by a simple wing-nut. These reels may or may not have U-shaped wire line guards. Being wood, plate and spool were liable to swell or warp when wet, and of course it was impossible to keep varnish on two surfaces that rubbed against each other. Later Nottingham reels were stiffened with brass straps across the frame plate, and these "star-back" reels can be very attractive—and reasonably priced—additions to any collection.

Historically, Nottinghams marked an important transition. At first—in their first century, let's say—they were used for many kinds of fishing, in both fresh and salt water, and hung both above and below the rod (depending, apparently, upon personal preference). Developmentally, Nottinghams led to click-type check and drag mechanisms and pillar-frame, center-spindle reels, but the original design survived easily also, and there is a strong mechanical resemblance to today's half-frame, exposed-rim fly reels such as the classic Orvis CFO. However, when Nottinghams ruled, bigger water and fish called for simply a larger reel—up to seven inches diameter, for example—and not a different reel. Specialization set in just after, especially in America.

The American equivalent of the Nottingham reel was the Kentucky reel, a highly refined offspring of the brass winches that had been brought over from England in the 18th century.

Kentucky was fertile soil in which to raise the fishing reel to new sophistication. At the turn of the 19th century it was civilized enough to be home for gunsmiths and other skilled mechanical tinkerers and craftsmen, and wild enough to provide sportfishing the like of which was fast disappearing in overpopulated Europe. George Snyder was likely the man who started it all, and he was a watchmaker and not a gunsmith. He didn't invent the multiplying reel, which came from Britain even before the American Revolution, but with his talent for fine machine work he elevated reel-making to an art. His reels, and those of his followers, including Benjamin Meek and his brother, Jonathan, of Frankfort, Kentucky, as well as J.L. Sage, B.C. Milam, and others, earned praise from sportsmen and outdoor writers for generations. Ben Meek later moved to Louisville, and with his two sons produced the renowned Blue Grass reels. These small Kentucky baitcasting reels, in production until the early 1900s, set new benchmarks for precision, function and quality, and are among the most desirable in the world.

However, for some reason (cultural differences between "country bumpkins" and "city slickers"?) most of the American reel patents issued in those years went not to Kentuckians but to inventors from New England and the Northeast. J.C. Conroy, Andrew Clark, Krider, J.B. Crook and others made similarly high-quality level-wind reels, mostly multipliers. Many carried the so-called "New York" style handle—a single handle at one end of a straight or S-curved crank, offset by a ball-shaped counterweight. Early Kentucky reels often had no handle counterbalance; later on, the weight was usually a stubby cylindrical plug mounted on a flat crank. Identifying the maker of some of these reels can sometimes be difficult, for they often were stamped only with a model or size number and the name of the store—Abbey & Imbrie, for example, or A.G. Spalding & Brothers—that sold them. To add to the confusion for collectors, some better-grade reels were often custom-engraved and bear only the name of the owner.

The mechanical improvements these men made in reels encompassed bearings, gears, clicks, and brake and drag mechanisms. Some went so far as to experiment with jeweled pivots (the watchmaking heritage, remember) for low friction, and about this time the compensating check came into use, a ratchet-and-pawl click system that adjusted itself for wear. Clicks had already been favored for many years as an audible warning signal when a fish began to take the bait, and on free-spool reels they also helped prevent overrunning and backlashes. The most common reel sizes held from 20 to about 50 yards of line, but some New York reels were made to hold as much as 200 yards of line heavy enough for Florida tarpon, a trophy that was attracting wealthy anglers from America and the Continent only 20 years after the Civil War.

CASTING a lure or bait by letting the line shoot through the rod guides probably dates from the early or mid-1800s. Reel authority Steven Vernon gives 1864 as the date of the first U.S. patent (issued to Andrew Dougherty of Brooklyn, New York) for a brake mechanism to keep a spinning spool from overrunning and tangling the line. Fly and bait fishermen had been pulling line off their reels (or unwinding it from sticks or even the rod butts) and then casting the loose coils for a century or more, but this likely marks the beginning of casting as most of us know it today—rod and reel working together, with line peeling directly off the reel and being taken up again right back onto the reel. For a brake to be needed, a clutch must already be in place, a way to disconnect the spool entirely from the machinery that retrieved the line. (Many fishermen also like to be able to free-spool line while fishing or even fish-fighting, not just while casting.)

Dougherty's brake, applied by a thumb lever, tightened a spring around a flange on the spinning spool to slow it down. However, the simplest way to control line backlash was, and still is, by direct thumb pressure on the revolving spool, and many manufacturers offered leather pads to attach to the rear pillar or foot of the reel, or even to wear as a thumb-thimble, to save a tender digit. For generations, expert casters have ignored or deactivated anti-backlash machinery because if it worked by itself it usually cut the casting distance appreciably. (By the late 1970s baitcasting reels commonly had magnetic brakes that slowed the spool from its maximum revolutions per minute; they worked pretty well with no input at all from the fisherman, but the experts routinely removed the little barrel magnets from their radial spindles anyway.)

At this point in the late 1800s, the hunt was well and truly on for reels that did everything—provided the least resistance to line during casting, and that could take up the most line while still offering fish-fighting control and a strong, highly adjustable drag. One way around the backlash/revolving spool headache was to ignore it entirely: Keep the spool fixed, and let line fly freely off one end of it. This is of course the idea behind the spinning reel. The concept, coupled much later with the development of thin nylon monofilament line, eventually helped make fishing something like the fourth largest recreational activity in America, and also helped bring about a crisis in American angling. Both came many years later, however.

In the States, a patent was issued in 1885 for the Winans & Whistler fixed-spool reel. It was mounted sideways on the rod, and line came out through a slot in its cover; to crank line back in, the cover flipped open and out of the way, and the angler turned the spool by means of its handle—which extended to the other side of the rod through a hole in its butt. It wasn't a commercial success, and closed-face spinning reels didn't become popular until some time after 1950. The most successful early "spinning" reel was a Scottish design, patented in the U.K. just a year earlier by Peter D. Malloch of Perth, a fisherman and caster of regional fame. It was unique in that the spool could be unlocked from its foot, rotated 90 degrees, and locked in place again. To cast, the spool stood parallel to the rod, and line uncoiled off it up through a built-in guide eye; the caster then flipped the spool perpendicular to the rod and simply turned it, via its crank, to wind line back in.

Incredibly, the Malloch's Spinning Reel stayed in production until World War II, evolving steadily and eventually offered in three sizes in aluminum as well as in "Gun Metal." It was a sturdy and an almost elegantly simple design, and today a Malloch's sidecaster is an excellent addition to any general reel collection. Good examples are still fairly easy to find, even in this country, and a very similar reel is currently in production by Alvey of Australia. It is very popular with surfcasters there because its huge spool diameter releases and retrieves line quickly, and its rugged construction—some spools are solid fiberglass—holds up well to the battering of down-under ocean fishing.

For all its strengths, the Malloch, like the coelacanth, was an evolutionary dead-end. Just after the turn of this century, an Englishman named Alfred Holden Illingworth began to manufacture his now-famous Thread Line Spinning Reel, and it was this design that went on to conquer the world. Like the Malloch, it had a vertical spool. Unlike the Malloch, its spool was fixed that way and, more important, the spool was cammed to rise and fall as the user turned the crank. The line went through a fixed wire loop, or bail, turned 90 degrees, and was wound more or less evenly onto the rotating spool, which in truth looked more like a sewing-machine bobbin than a reel spool. (Today, of course, it is the bail that revolves while the spool stays fixed.) Despite its somewhat ungainly appearance, any modern fisherman would recognize the earliest Illingworth instantly as a "real" spinning reel—even though Illingworth himself originally patented his creation as a "Bait Casting Reel." (The term "spinning" was, however, already in use, thanks to Malloch.) Illingworth reels stayed in production until late in the 1930s, and were steadily improved along the way. An Illingworth No. 3, for example, which received a U.S. patent in 1916, is visually almost a dead ringer for a contemporary spinning reel except that it lacks a folding bail.

Spin-fishing didn't really hit its stride in the States until after World War II. Then, the combined socio-economic effects of 1) thousands of de-mobilized men flooding back into America 2) the shift from a rural to a "nine-to-five" economy, with new leisure time for recreation and 3) the war-induced economic boom rocked every aspect of life in the United States. Sportfishing—or rather sport*fish*—were hard hit, and the spinning reel contributed heavily. The important factor was that casting with a spinning reel is dead easy, while mastering a level-wind baitcasting reel or fly tackle is comparatively harder. As a result, more inexperienced fishermen could cover more water than ever before.

After the war, DuPont rushed nylon monofilament onto the market, and this superbly light yet strong fishing line was just what the spinning reel needed. Fifty years before, Alfred Illingworth knew what he was doing when he called his invention the Thread Line reel; he recognized immediately that, because of its essentially frictionless line delivery, a spinning reel could cast finer lines farther than any other tackle. It took that long, however, for line technology to catch up with reel design.

(Did you know that even today there are people at DuPont who insist that "Nylon" is in fact an acronym for "Now you look out, Nippon?" After the Japanese took Burma, synthetic rubber and other plastics became vital to the war effort.) At about the same time, inexpensive, highly functional fiberglass rods went into mass-production for all kinds of fishing. And the excellent French-made Mitchell spinning reels, imported by Garcia, became the choice of many of our new fishermen in the 1950s, despite their high price. As outdoor recreation boomed, these and other elements came together, and suddenly fresh-water and coastal fish had no place left to hide. The manufacture of fish hooks, specialized lures, lead sinkers, tackle boxes, landing nets, car-top boats, outboard motors, utility and four-wheel-drive vehicles, camping equipment, and so on also boomed. Lakes began to get crowded. Surfcasting, previously restricted to experts who could "thumb" big level-wind reels with awesome precision, suddenly opened up, and the newcomers with spinning gear could often outcast the old-timers. (Newcomers using the new soft plastic worms, invented in 1949 by an Ohio machinist named Nick Creme, could often outfish the old-timers, too.) Even stream trout—previously the target mostly of fly fishermen, who couldn't yet fish very effectively below the surface of the current—were now exposed: weighted lures or hooks on ultrafine, nearly invisible monofilament lines could cut down through the fast water and reach into the hidey-holes where trout sought cover, and the slaughter was on.

It took decades and many generations of gamefish for America's fish & game laws, as well as our code of outdoor ethics, to catch up with this relatively swift shift in the sport. Strict bag limits, catch-and-release fishing, "limit your kill, don't kill your limit," controlled no-kill waters, fish-for-pay, the scientific study of fish habitat and lifecycles . . . all these concepts arrived barely in the nick of time. One might argue that the spinning reel worked too well, but today these vast numbers of fishermen are becomingly increasingly conservation-minded and, ironically, may yet prove to be the salvation of our gamefish and our waters.

AS THE spinning reel branched off onto its own limb of the fishing-tackle family tree, the "old-fash-ioned" rotating-spool, winch-type reel progressed very nicely also, encompassing fly reels, big-game and trolling reels, and the bass fisherman's baitcasting type, each in many different sizes. After the Civil War, American reel manufacturing entered what many collectors today regard as its Nirvana stage, when names such as Follet, Orvis, Billinghurst, Leonard, Chubb, Vom Hofe and Meisselbach joined the Kentucky and New York crowd.

The distinction between fly-fishing and other sorts of angling had been drawn centuries before, and the key to it was that the "baits" and thus the lines had to be different. That is, to cast an essentially weightless bait—a hook dressed with feathers or fur—the line had to provide the mass; this is the converse of spinning, where a weight at the end of the line—the lure—pulled the relatively weightless line out with it during casting. However, the setting-apart of fly *reels* became important after (to pick a date as meaningful as any) 1859. That was the year the Billinghurst "birdcage" reel was issued a patent, and it ushered in the era of the American narrow-frame (that is, taller than it was wide), ventilated-spool fly reel.

The advantage of a narrow-frame, deep-spool reel was that it could have a fairly thick arbor, or center, on which the line was wound. Furthermore, as the line piled up on the narrow arbor, the effective spool diameter broadened quickly. Both features increased the amount of line that a turn of the crank brought in, and without any possibly temperamental gear drives. Reel makers also discovered that by locating the crank handle right on the spool itself, nearer or farther from the reel's center, they could vary the fisherman's mechanical advantage. The single-action (one-to-one retrieve ratio) fly reel of today is essentially the same as that developed in the middle years of the 19th century.

The ventilated spool lightened a reel and, more important, improved air circulation and thus speeded up drying of the delicate braided silk fly lines of the day, which would mildew and rot if left damp. Still today, many fly fishermen refuse to buy reels that are not ventilated, even though modern synthetic lines shrug water off (and should be protected from sunlight, if anything); a solid-spool type just doesn't "look like a fly reel."

The streamlined, skeletal Billinghurst reel, with its wire cage spool and its folding single handle, was quite modern in about every respect, except that it mounted horizontally on the rod. So did its design successor, the similarly rare and valuable Gem reel. In his exhaustive *Fishing Reel Patents of the United States 1838-1940*, Jim Brown writes, "Dr. Alonzo Fowler, a dentist from Ithaca, New York, used the molding technology of his trade to design a hard-rubber reel that was patented on June 18, 1872.

Fowler's Gem, as the reel was called, represents one of the earliest uses of hard rubber in the construction of fishing reels." (Charles Goodyear received the first of the rubber patents that made this possible in 1851.) The Gem, with its modern-looking but exposed click and pawl, its minimal half-frame, and its drilled, eggshell-thin Vulcanite (as hard rubber was called) spool, was too fragile to be a big success. But, with the Billinghurst, it pointed the way toward such modern "gems" as The Orvis Company's CFO family of reels.

That company, in the person of founder Charles F. Orvis (hence "CFO"), gave us the next step in fly reels: the famous Orvis Trout Reel, of 1874 patent. Design-wise, it was a trend-setter, almost exaggeratedly narrow. It was made of German silver (nickel-silver) or nickel-plated brass, and both frame and spool were radically drilled; it mounted vertically on the rod and boasted a click mechanism; and it eventually came in different spool widths, with a plain or a counterbalanced S-shaped crank handle, and was screwed together instead of rivetted.

Company records show that by the turn of the century production switched over to aluminum, which is still the material of choice for fly reels today. Light, strong aluminum had previously been almost a precious metal; but as breakthroughs came in refining bauxite, the cost of aluminum dropped dramatically. After 1900, it became increasingly common in fishing reels, and this, like the patent date of hard rubber, can serve as a quick yardstick for dating an unknown reel.

Seen from 20 feet or so, an 1874 Orvis is almost indistinguishable from a modern trout reel, except perhaps by its bright, polished finish, which few anglers would tolerate today because of the potential for trout-spooking reflections. The reel was accepted immediately, sold briskly, and joined Orvis rods and flies in propelling the company to the top of the American fly fisher's hit parade. No fly reel collection—in fact, no historical reel collection—is complete without an 1874-patent Orvis. Not only is it important, it also came in a handsome fitted walnut case that shows it off to great advantage.

As the marvelous six-strip bamboo fly rod neared perfection, the search heightened for ways to make fly reels lighter, stronger, and more functional. Nothing was more significant than the Orvis reel, but a design detail of importance to reel collectors was the raised-pillar frame. Raised-pillar reels have their frame crossbars above, or outside, the spool, for maximum line capacity at minimum weight. Reel expert Jim Brown (*Fishing Reel Patents of the United States 1838-1940*) identifies a fly reel patented by James Ross in 1869 as perhaps the first American raised-pillar design, but it was Francis J. Philbrook, of Bangor, Maine, who popularized the idea. He assigned his patent (issued June 12, 1877) to Hiram Leonard, the bamboo-rod pioneer, who then also lived and worked in Bangor. Philbrook manufactured the reels with Edward Payne (himself to become one of America's greatest rod makers), and Leonard sold them. When Leonard joined the New York tackle firm of Wm. Mills & Son, the reel was then sold under the name "Leonard-Mills." Philbrook and Payne split up in 1884, and Philbrook went on making reels until his death in '88. The Leonard-Mills reel was eventually produced in the Vom Hofe shop in New York, and it became immensely popular with anglers of that day and with collectors of today. Raised-pillar reels have apparently become something of a symbol. When basement machinist Bill Ballan began making a limited number of his "Classic" raised-pillar trout reels in 1988, they immediately sold for more than their list price at auction and in private sales.

Many collectors and tackle historians regard the Vom Hofe family as the Wyeths of the reel business. Edward Vom Hofe & Company was established in 1867; Edward's brother, Julius, also became a reel maker; both men, however, were but following in the footsteps of the father, Frederick, and Vom Hofe reels stayed in production until World War II. In their familial competiton to make the best, the Vom Hofes developed clicks, drag systems and adjusters, multiplying gears, and sizes and proportions that have never been surpassed and rarely equalled. (One company motto was, "They never wear out.") The Vom Hofes offered many models, including bait and trolling reels, but their name is forever linked with fly reels. The most prized are the Perfection, first known as the Celebrated Trout and Bass Fly Reel; the Salmon and Grilse Click Reel, later dubbed the Restigouche; and the Multiplying Salmon Reel, re-christened the Tobique. They were all made in an almost bewildering range of sizes, both with and without "silent tension drag."

After the war, a former employee named Otto Zwarg went on making Vom Hofe-style reels, using leftover parts when he could, and applying the names of other famous salmon rivers to them. The famous English firm, Hardy Bros., patterned some of its salmon models after the Vom Hofes. Then another fine reel maker named Arthur Walker entered the picture with similar reels, and today's Bogdan reels (and the newer Godfreys, Saracione "Classics" and likely others) continue to pay homage to the engineering and design genius of the Vom Hofe family.

BECAUSE of their sheer size and strength, as well as the meticulous machine work that they display, the most impressive fishing tackle are the huge trolling reels used offshore for bluefin tuna, the great billfish and the game sharks. Their development had to wait for a demand, naturally, and this didn't come about until well into this century.

According to Jack Samson, former editor of *Field & Stream*, true big-game fishing traces back on the West Coast to June 1, 1898, when a Mr. Charles F. Holder boated a bluefin tuna near Catalina Island that weighed 183 pounds. Within a matter of weeks, there was a tuna club in place there, and two dozen members had caught fish of a hundred pounds or more. In the East the Florida tarpon had already became the big-game fish of choice, after W.H. Wood took an 81-pounder and a 93-pounder on the same day, March 25, 1885. Tarpon had been caught before, of course, but these fish were highly publicized, and the rush was on. (Wood went on, later that year, to gaff a fish that was over 100 pounds; 10 years later, also in Florida, England's Lady Orford became the first recorded woman to take two tarpon in one day, one of them said to have weighed 128 pounds.) These fish were landed on oversize freshwater reels made by Vom Hofe, Conroy and others. Perhaps some of the so-called Indiana reels were also pressed into saltwater service–large skeletal-frame reels made in the late 1800s for trolling in deepwater lakes.

Big-game tackle began to be taken very seriously in 1913, when William Boschen, of New York City, landed the first known broadbill swordfish on a rod. The reel contained a heavy-duty, anti-reverse clutch and drag system that Boschen, fittingly enough, had designed himself and then taken to Julius Vom Hofe to have built. Then, in 1924, Zane Grey set the angling world on its ear by killing a 758-pound bluefin tuna off Yarmouth, Nova Scotia.

Grey, author of the famous series of best-selling western novels, was a multimillionaire sportsman who spared no expense in his hunts for the finest fishing the globe had to offer. To him, a thousand Depression-era dollars (or more) for the right fishing reel was a pittance–especially compared to the cost of owning and operating his specially equipped 186-foot world-girdling fishing boat. For a while he was a devotee of the elegantly simple and strong trolling reels built by J.A. Coxe. In the early 1930s, the British firm Hardy Bros. honored him by introducing its "Zane Grey" line of ultimate big-game reels.

(Any early Hardy Zane Grey is a collector's piece. The series went out of production before World War II, but new Zane Greys were introduced, on essentially a custom-order basis, around 1980. Tomorrow's collector's item?)

The most intriguing big-game reels of all, however, are probably the rim-control models built for Grey in the '30s by Californian Arthur Kovalovsky. They are massively built and cleverly engineered, and they helped Grey set a number of world records, including the 1,036-pound tiger shark that was the first fish ever taken on rod and reel to exceed a thousand pounds. Kovalovsky himself was a very unusual man. He was born in Hungary in 1881, apprenticed as a metalsmith, and emigrated to the U.S.A. in 1904. He became, naturally enough, a skilled engine mechanic and worked on those new-fangled devices called automobiles and airplanes. While still relying on automotive repairs for his living, he made his first fishing reels in 1928, then three years later went into the reel business full-time. Although "production" (the reels were really hand-made, in very small lots) continued, off and on, into the 1950s, virtually any Kovalovsky reel is a collector's item today.

Tycoon Fin-Nor builds what are regarded as the best offshore reels of today, but a New Jersey company called Angling Products, Inc. signed an agreement in 1987 with Oscar Kovalovsky, Arthur's son, himself in his 80s, to produce a new series of "ultimate" reels of his design. These, for both fly-fishing and big game, are as over-engineered as the father's reels were, and as beautifully made. The limited-production fly reels already command steep prices, and if the trolling reel ever appears, it is likely to set a new standard among big-game anglers.

IT IS SIMPLY not possible to mention here the dozens, or maybe even hundreds, of reels worthy of the collector's admiration and attention. Names such as Horton, Atwood, Pflueger, Shakespeare (who popularized the level-wind mechanism), Hendryx, Heddon, Yawman & Erbe, Martin, Diamond, Penn and many others have not even been mentioned. Both Hardy's and Meisselbach deserve a chapter of their own in any history of fishing reels. We've hardly scratched the surface of the myriad types of gear drives, drag systems and construction techniques that make reels so fascinating to the collector—not to mention the hundreds of sometimes confusing and conflicting patents that their inventors took out. We have left out all mention of automatic reels, a collecting category unto themselves, and we've not even tried to describe any of reel-building's true oddities—such as the Phillips' "surfcasting catapult," a highly impractical combination crossbow and spear launcher designed to fire a lure over the surf line, or William Stuart's intriguing "built-in," a geared reel hidden within the butt of its rod. The beginning collector should, however, be aware of all of these. He or she should also be able to place his reels within their own social and cultural times, for we and our artifacts are no more and no less than products of those times.

Valuable, desirable, collectible reels are still being produced as you read this. Consider the phenomenon of the fly reels made today by Stanley Bogdan of Nashua, New Hampshire, and Robert ("Captain Mac") MacChristian of Miami, who builds the Seamaster reels. Both gentlemen started in the business in the 1940s and both continue to produce reels in their small machine shops today.

Their work is nearly flawless, and they and their products have had decades in which to make their mark and earn their reputations in top sportfishing grounds—the world's salmon rivers and its bone-fish and tarpon flats. As Stan Bogdan and Capt. Mac grow older, their production inevitably slows down (even though both men are training sons or grandsons to take over)—while demand increases as more and more of us "discover" them.

In the late 1980s, when brand-new Bogdan salmon and trout reels and Seamaster saltwater fly reels were selling at retail for about $500 to $650, depending on model and size, excellent previously owned versions of the same reels brought up to $2,000 and more at tackle auctions and in private sales. An engraved Atlantic Salmon Federation commemorative Bogdan sold for slightly more than $4,000 in August, 1988. The buyers were sportsmen unwilling to wait three to five years to have their orders filled at the factory, or they were serious, investment-minded collectors who foresaw continually climbing prices. A non-antique—in fact, a current-production—item had become a wildly sought-after collectable.

ASSORTED TROLLING, casting, spinning, spincasting and fly reels—part of one dealer's offerings at the RWO Auction swap meet. Several very fine and highly desirable reels surfaced on these tables.

PROSPECTIVE BIDDERS, catalogs in hand, examine the lots on one of the reel tables as preview time winds down before the annual RWO Classic Tackle Auction.

HEADING FOR the auction block: A Vom Hofe salmon fly reel (top); a large wind-up automatic fly reel by Yawman & Erbe, and several British fly reels, including, at bottom, a Hardy.

CLASSIC BRITISH NOTTINGHAM REELS.
Clockwise from top: An unmarked four-inch star-back reel with shiny varnish and ivory handles • A well-appointed version, with a heavy wire "Bickerdyke" line guide and a sliding click button set into the brass star frame • A very basic Nottingham, typical of the hundreds that turn up at tackle flea markets; this one has bone handles.

AN EXTREMELY rare and valuable J.L. Sage No.2 trout or baitcasting reel made of German silver. It measures a mere 1 5/8 inches in diameter and has a 1 3/8-inch-wide spool. Sage, who began making reels in about 1881 and died in 1897, achieved a lifetime production of only some 300 reels. Of them, Dr. James Henshall, author of The Book of the Black Bass and the "father of modern baitcasting," said "I have the smallest and neatest 'Kentucky reel' I have ever seen; it was made by Mr. Sage."

ANOTHER FINE Kentucky reel—a c.1890 B.C. Milam No.4, handmade in German silver, with an ivory handle and click and drag buttons. Both ends of the foot have at one time been filed down, to fit a particular rod seat, and this decreases the reel's value.

A BRASS Elkhorn production baitcasting reel by "S. Meek, Frankfort, KY." Sylvanius was Benjamin Meek's son, also a reel maker. The reel has drag and click buttons on the back and shows traces of nickel plating.

A HANDMADE German-silver B.C. Milam Kentucky baitcasting reel,
serial #7207, with click and drag buttons, an ivory handle, and an early
long foot.

AN UNUSUAL "B.F. Meek & Sons, Louisville, KY" reel, marked "Club Special" on the front, serial #2103, and specially engraved on the back: "Mrs. Robt. T. Kochs Chicago". It is a No.2 size—1 5/8-inch diameter—but has a 1 3/4-inch spool. Also jeweled bearings, an ivory handle, and a sliding click button.

A RELATIVELY scarce Bluegrass No.4 German-silver baitcasting reel made by B.F. Meek & Sons, Louisville, KY. Serial number is #2907 and it has jeweled bearings and sliding click and drag buttons. On the back is engraved "J.T. Roby Elizabethtown Oct. 10, 1866, Apr. 1907." The leather case is original.

A PLAIN but very rare and valuable "B.F. Meek & Sons, Louisville, KY No.44" German-silver fly reel, 2 1/4 inches in diameter. The rear view shows the sliding click button and removable bearing cap. It was likely made between 1905 and 1910.

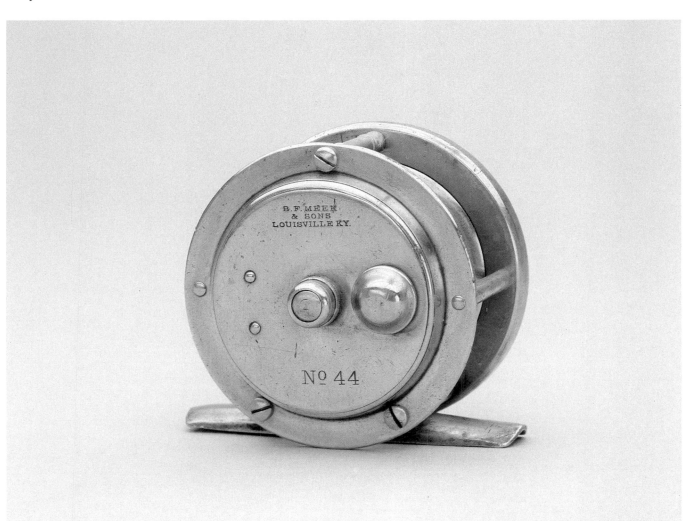

NOT SO *very rare, but an excellent example of a premier salmon reel is this large (6/0 size) Edward Vom Hofe "Restigouche" in its original "Mills N.Y." case. Originally called the Salmon and Grilse Click Reel, the Restigouche, like the Perfection, was made of German silver, hard rubber, and aluminum, and came in a variety of sizes, with a click and with or without the Vom Hofe "silent tension drag."*

A FINE *pair of Meek free-spooling tournament reels, both with aluminum spools and "cork wood" arbors, and both made by "The Horton Mfg. Co., Bristol, Conn." The tiny No.2 is serial #11425; the No.3, with its unusual triple-handle crank, bears #12011.*

NEW YORK "ball-handle" reels, of approximately Civil-War vintage. The brass reel is stamped "J.C. Conroy & Co N.Y." and it has the early dome-shaped bearing cover on the back plate and an offset foot. The other reel, three inches in diameter, is made of nickel-plated German silver and bears the markings "Onion, Haigh & Cornwall N.Y."

AN EARLY Illingworth No.3 spinning reel with exposed gear train and original fitted fiberboard case.

PERHAPS THE rarest of all American fly reels is this first-model Billinghurst "birdcage," patented in 1859. Of brass, 3 1/4 inches in diameter, it is a centermount type with a folding wooden handle. What really sets this particular one apart, however, is that it appears to be still "new in the box"—the cardboard container is the only one known to exist.

THIS UNUSED 1960s Mitchell No. 403 high-speed-retrieve salt-water spinning reel is complete in its box with spare spool, warranty papers, and takedown tool; that assures it of some value even today, before it becomes scarce.

ONE OF the famous Malloch Patent fixed-spool sidecast spinning reels, beautifully made and still loaded (with modern line) and ready for action. This is a large and fairly early version, with the Gibbs locking lever and a click button. The eccentric button on top is a spool release.

AN UNUSUAL and rare sidemount baitcasting reel marked "Waltonian Casting Reel M'f'd by Square Stamping Co. Inc. Barneveld, N.Y. Cap. 100 yds. Pat. Pending". The frame is German silver, with an aluminum spool gear-driven by the off-center crank. Pushing on the "stirrup" declutches the reel (separates the drive gears) for free-spooling.

AN EARLY *riveted example of the classic Orvis 1874 ventilated fly reel, 2 3/4 inches in diameter. Note the cut-out in the walnut case for the detachable crank. Marked "C.F. Orvis Maker Manchester, Vt. Patented May 12th, 1874."*

A SPECTACULAR example of an original raised-pillar trout reel clearly stamped "Philbrook & Payne" and "H.L. Leonard Maker"— even though Edward Payne likely built the reel. The raised-pillar design was patented by Philbrook and Payne in 1877 and then assigned to Hiram Leonard for marketing. Such reels with their full markings intact are very rare, for the "marbleized" rubber sideplates are relatively soft and wear easily. The handle is hard rubber and the frame German silver. The reel is greatly enlarged here; it measures only two inches in diameter.

More valuable still would be a reel in similar condition marked "Philbrook & Payne Pat. Pending" or with no patent inscription at all—thus pre-June 12, 1877. At least three of these are known to survive.

DR. ALONZO FOWLER'S centermount "Gem" trout reel, patented in June 1872. Its hard-rubber spool has over the years taken on a bronze patina, and it is almost eggshell fragile. This is the smaller, 40-yard-capacity model, 2 3/4 inches in diameter. Five examples are thought to survive, of which two are in museums.

A PAIR OF SEMI-SKELETAL TROUT REELS.
Left: a rare 1887-patent No.3 (2 7/8-inch diameter) Pettengill marked "A. Pettengill Pat. P'D'G". The other is a side-mount 3 5/8-inch Follet complete with its original handle; equally rare, it dates from the 1880s.

RAISED-PILLAR LEONARD REELS.

Left to right: A four-inch salmon reel stamped "H.L. Leonard Pat. No. 191813" with a sliding drag adjuster at the top of the back plate and a leather case marked "Mills, N.Y." • A rare first model Bi-Metal Trout reel, stamped "H.L. Leonard Pat. June 12, 1877", the Philbrook & Payne patent date. German silver and bronze, it is 2 3/8 inches in diameter • An early "Leonard-Mills" Midge click reel. Only 2 1/8 inches in diameter, it has aluminum spool flanges and frame rims • A fancy four-inch salmon reel, also marked with the Philbrook & Payne "Pat. No. 191813," and with the monogram "GMB" engraved on both the reel and its "Mills" leather case. The sliding drag regulator is at the bottom of the sideplate • A Trout click model, marked "Leonard-Mills". At 2 3/4 inches, it is a larger version of the Midge.

SMALL TROUT REELS.
Clockwise from top: A silent late-1800s brass reel with fishing scenes in raised relief on both sides; diameter is 2 1/2 inches • A rare Malleson multiplier with a bullet handle and center-mounted, counterbalanced crank—the gear drive is in a housing on the rear plate. The arrowhead indicator flips back and forth with each click. Marked "Patented by Fred'k Malleson, Sept. 4, 83" • A tiny (1 7/8-inch) single-action reel made by T.H. Chubb, its value diminished only by its condition • Another scarce Chubb, this one measuring two inches across, with a smooth sideplate and most of its nickel finish intact.

THE CLASSIC, highly desirable Edward Vom Hofe "Perfection" trout fly reel (top) set the standard for all others that followed its 1896 patent date. This is a No.1, three inches in diameter, with hard rubber sideplates and German silver and aluminum components. The red dots and pointer indicate the drag setting. To the left is a smaller Perfection trout model, the No.3.

The two small trout reels are both by Julius Vom Hofe; the bone-handled version, with its counterweighted crank, is marked "Abbey & Imbrie N.Y."; the other was sold by "Dame, Stoddard, Kendall, Boston." They measure respectively, two and 2 1/4 inches in diameter.

A PAIR of Edward Vom Hofe multiplying salmon reels.
The 2/0 size "Tobique" (left) and a three-inch-diameter "Col. Thompson
Dri-Fly," the rarest and probably the most valuable of all the Vom Hofe
salmon reels. Its patent marking is 1883, but these reels were produced for
only a short time in the 1920s. This one is number 484.

A HANDSOME pair of turn-of-the-century heavy salmon reels, both 4
1/2 inches in diameter. The reel on the left is stamped "Thos. J. Conroy,
N.Y. Maker," with a classic "bullet" handle mounted on an ornately
counterbalanced crank. The black hard-rubber sideplates have acquired a
deep bronze hue. The other reel boasts a brass spool with integral crank
knob, and hard-rubber sideplates and silver rims. Its maker is unknown.

HARDY FLY REELS.
Left to right: A very rare multiplying/expanded-spool St. George, 3 3/8-inch diameter, with its gear drive in the awkward-looking housing. The foot is grooved brass • A pre-WWII 3 5/8-inch Perfect "Duplicated Mk II" with bright finish and a grooved brass foot • Another 3 5/8-inch Perfect, this one with the scarce Compensating Check drag; it also has a guard over the tension adjuster, a smooth brass foot, and an agate ring line guide. (Although "typical" Perfects carry ring-type guides, lined with agate or metal, not all have them—very early Perfects, which date back to 1891, carried wire guides; some later "modern" Perfects have no guide at all) • A massive blued-finish Salmon Perfect, Duplicated Mk II, 4 1/2 inches in diameter; the metal line guide rotates, to distribute wear.

THIS MASSIVE (17 pounds) stainless-steel trolling reel is one of the finest examples of the work of Hollywood reel maker Arthur Kovalovski, who hand-built it in about 1935, apparently for wealthy angler/author Joseph Conrad. It is stamped "Kovalovski-Zane Grey" on its handle and front rim; the foot is marked "No.18," and the back plate bears the words "Joseph Conrad Charleston, S.C., U.S.A."

The frame measures some nine inches wide and is about 7 1/2 inches in diameter. The four-level "wedding-cake" construction on the crank side of the frame incorporates a large rim-control brake, with its complex linkages and handle knob, an adjustable free-spool setting, and a high-capacity oil reservoir. On the back plate is a large sliding oil cover and an on-off click switch. Kovalovski designed and built a number of reels for Zane Grey, and Grey reportedly convinced Conrad, who was also fishing in Australia in 1935, that he too should have such a machine.

The German-silver plaque on the handle butt is engraved "Designed & built by Arthur Kovalovski Hollywood, Cal. Hand Made." The two mating rod tips that attach to the butt still exist, and are in equally good condition.

HARDY FLY reels. Clockwise from top: An exposed-rim 2 3/4-inch Sunbeam fitted with a brass wire line guide and foot • A 3 1/8-inch Uniqua, "Duplicated Mk II," with a grooved brass foot and a straight— as opposed to crescent—spool latch. • A Birmingham-type brass trout reel, 2 1/2-inch diameter, with a bone handle • A rare early Hardy Hercules brass reel, also 2 1/2 inches across, with an ivorine handle; this one is engraved "MARY FIRTH". The latter two are 19th-Century models, with Hardy's old rod-in-hand logo.

VOM HOFE saltwater reels. Top: Julius Vom Hofe B-Ocean saltwater reel, in 4/0 size, marked with the retailer's name, "Thos. J. Conroy N.Y." (The leather case is also marked Conroy.) A leather thumb brake pad is attached to the rear frame pillar. The reel on the left is a No. 550 "Star" 3/0 surfcasting reel, by Julius's brother, Edward Vom Hofe; it bears a 1902 patent date. The third reel, also an Edward Vom Hofe, is a scarce and particularly beautiful No. 650 "Islamorada" surfcasting model. Only three inches in diameter, with an 1896 patent date, it features a rare rotary drag adjuster on its back plate and a very stylish ventilated star drag wheel.

The catalog, 171 pages or reels, rods, lures and angling supplies, is the company's thirty-first edition.

THE FULL-SIZE (2 3/4-inch dia.) trout reel is an out-of-production *Shakespeare International 2850*, with a full cage frame and a palming rim on the spool. Although it was a product of a mass-market tackle company, the reel was fully machined from magnesium, and its value is now climbing. The functional miniature reel measures 15/16 of an inch across and boasts a click; it was made by a contemporary British jeweler.

A LARGE—six-inch diameter—J.A. Coxe handmade big-game reel that belonged to best-selling author and world-girdling angler Zane Grey. In his 1927 book *Tales of Swordfish & Tuna*, Grey described this reel: "I had constructed for me the famous Coxe reel, much larger than the 9/0, and it cost fifteen hundred dollars." Sixty-five years later, in July 1988, the reel sold at auction for a surprisingly low $6,600—a substantial devaluation, in adjusted dollars.

A HIGHLY unusual assortment of Bogdan salmon reels.
Left to right: A 3 5/8-inch multiplier with a white plastic handle, an unusual steel plate attached under the crank, and (just visible) a rare one-
pillar sleeve-type line guide • A gold-anodized No.300 multiplier • A
gold No.200 multiplier on its original Abercrombie & Fitch box (new, in
the 1950s, it sold for $100) • A Bogdan No.50 Salmon Steelhead reel,
distinguished by its ventilated frame and single-action works • A 3 5/8-
inch multiplier with a one-inch-wide spool; set up for left-hand winding, it
has a rare double-post (only one turns) line guide. Engraved on the front
plate is "GORDON SHIRRES".

NOT ALL collectible reels bring five-figure prices. This large Winona No.30 wire-line model, while of no historical significance at all, is typical of outdated, unusual designs that demonstrate the great variety of fishing reels.

TOMORROW'S VALUED COLLECTIBLES?
A pair of older Pflueger Medalist fly reels. On the left is an early 1495½ with an aluminum spool hub cap and a ring-type line guide. The other is a model 1496½. Though not of the same mechanical sophistication, Medalists have attained about the same warm spot in the hearts of American fly fishermen that Hardy Perfects have with their British counterparts.

HANDMADE IN NASHUA, NEW HAMPSHIRE. *These are contemporary fly reels built by Stan Bogdan, shown on their leather bags. On the left and below are scarce "Baby Trout" models, 2 5/8 inches in diameter— the wide version (left) has a one-inch spool, while the narrow-spool model is only half an inch wide. The third reel is a standard 3 1/8x3/4-inch Trout. All are highly desirable and equally functional.*

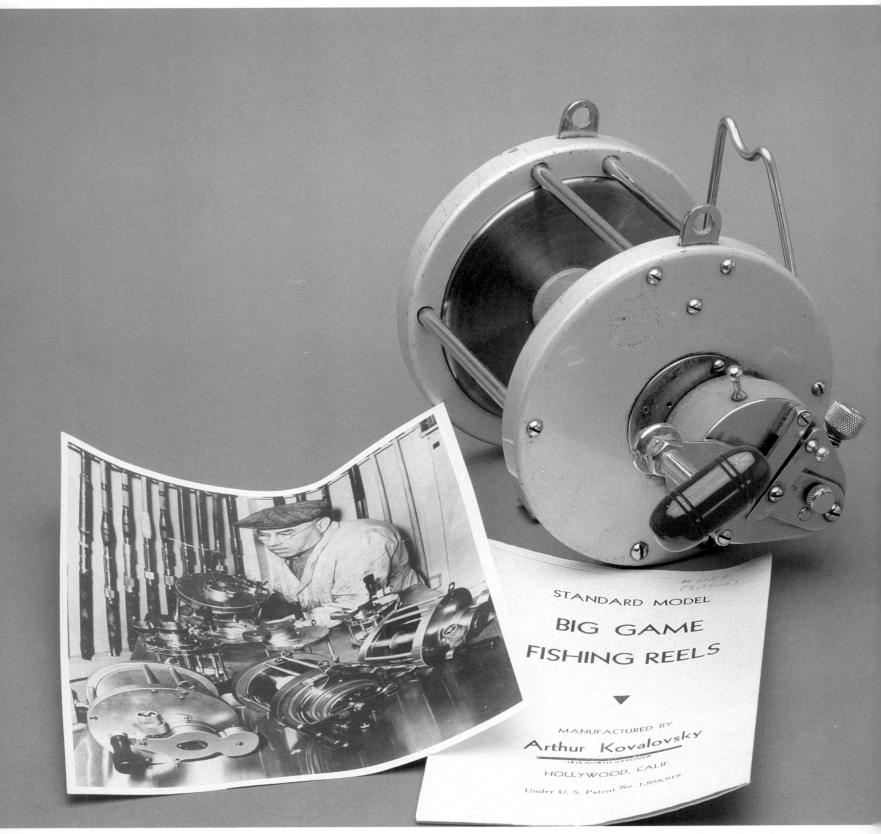

STANDARD MODEL

BIG GAME
FISHING REELS

▼

MANUFACTURED BY

Arthur Kovalovsky

1515 NORTH GARDNER

HOLLYWOOD, CALIF.

Under U. S. Patent No. 1,958,919

AN INTRICATE 14/0 Kovalovski big-game reel: 6 1/4 inches in diameter, with a four-inch-wide spool. The photo shows Oscar Kovalovski in his California shop, probably in the '30s. Compared to the Vom Hofe-style hard-rubber and German-silver Coxe reels of a decade earlier, this one, with its bright handle and brush-finish sideplates, looks quite modern. The reel belonged to the Grey family, but is thought to have been used by Romer, Zane's son.

AN EARLY Fin-Nor #1 saltwater/salmon fly reel of the scarce and sought-after "wedding-cake" style. This particular example is serial #27 and bears an escutcheon plate engraved "G.R. FORD". If it can be traced positively to President Gerald R. Ford, its value will only increase.

THE FAMOUS Bogdan twin-shoe floating salmon drag, operated by the dual eccentric cam at right. Every component save these springs and a few internal screws are made entirely by Stan Bogdan and his son, Steve. The sideplate at the rear shows a spool multiplier-drive gear.

A SIGNIFICANT Hardy Zane Grey six-inch big-game reel, complete with its original linen line. The accessories include a turnbuckle-type rod clamp, an oiler, and a grease gun, as well as the leather case that housed everything. The case top is decorated with Grey's personal colors and the inscription "To Romer, from Dad, Zane Grey"; Grey's signature appears inside as well. The reel also bears the Grey colors.

The Zane Grey items in this book were all part of a collection assembled by a man named Huck Spawr, who bought (from a dealer) items that were sold by Romer and other family members to raise money after Zane's death. Parts of the Huck Spawr Collection have recently been sold off in turn.

LURES

THE SCREWBALL side of fishing comes perilously close to the surface when one delves into the history of lures–the word in this case used to mean flies, plugs, spoons, worms, teasers, trolling chains and the other artificial baits meant to entice fish to their doom. In fact, one need not even "delve" at all. A non-angler with a thoughtful bent, strolling the aisles of a well-stocked specialty fishing shop, would see to the heart of the looniness right away: Can all these different lures really be necessary to catch a simple-minded eating machine like a fish? Or is it that they are perhaps designed in this endless variety to catch fishermen too?

The fishermen, however, on a similar recon through a shop generally miss this observation entirely, and some would likely be insulted (mildly, anyway) to have it pointed out to them. We are, after all, supposed to be smarter than the fish. The reason, we might respond, for using different shapes, colors, materials, sizes, hook and eye configurations, diving lips, beads, spinners, wiggly appendages, noise-makers, scents, and even artificial lights is that gamefish have learning curves. Show a largemouth bass, for example, the same lure too often, and it will try to murder it–or ignore it forever. Hook the fish on one, and it may never again strike *any* artificial bribe. And everyone appreciates a little variety in the menu, no?

The stereotypical fly fisherman–there must be one left, somewhere–when asked if the 16,000-plus recognizable fly patterns identified worldwide are truly needed, might puff on his briar and speak learnedly of "matching the hatch" and of the legendary finickiness of his traditional quarry, the trout and salmon, bonefish and tarpon. There is absolutely no question that a closer imitation of a natural insect or baitfish can often draw more strikes; however, almost as often, an oddball pattern will get a rush out of a fish also, even in the midst of plentiful real food.

One of the most widely appreciated kinds of collectible tackle is classic salmon flies, especially the patterns that are tied with as many as two dozen different feathers and hairs, threads and tinsels, and that may take an hour and a half to "dress" properly. They are often breathtakingly beautiful constructions, approaching fine jewelry in their design, proportion, color and craftsmanship. Bitter arguments have erupted again and again over whether a particular fly is a true recreation of the original, and the assumption by the casual observer is that this accuracy is a vital matter to the salmon, which may–or may not–turn its nose up at it. Isn't that what fishing is about?

Nothing could be further from the truth. The salmon in its spawning river doesn't eat any natural food for as long as eight months or so, and furthermore most of these flies resemble no living thing. Many of the classic patterns were created by Irish and Scottish ghillies, who eked out their meager farm incomes by tying flies for the gentry they guided on the salmon beats in season. It's likely there was some competition among these characters to make flies that outshone those of their rivals, and so would sell better. Giving them names like Tup's Indispensable and Greenwell's Glory probably didn't hurt sales either.

An eye-catching lure or fly that was marketed well was likely to end up being used by more fishermen, and statistically would catch more fish. This then led to a reputation as a fish-getter, which redoubled its sales, and so on until that particular fad was somehow eclipsed by the next hot item. I don't mean to be overly cynical here; for me, part of the charm of antique lures lies exactly in this somewhat charming blend of craft and craftsmanship. Like the legendary better mousetrap, the better fishing lure catches as many fishermen as it does fish.

THE BASIC ingredient of a lure is the hook. In ancient times, or today in plentiful and unspoiled fisheries, the hook often *was* the lure–no extra enticement was needed. The historian of the venerable Mustad hook-making company, Hans Jørgen Hurum, writes that the earliest hooks were likely made of wood, sections of branch with sharpened, and often fire-hardened, twigs protruding at tactical angles. Coastal Alaskan natives caught huge halibut with wooden hooks that were reinforced with lashings of sinew and often carved like miniature totem poles, with fanciful heads and faces. Other "natural" fish hooks included the beaks and claws of birds of prey; carved sections of bone, tusk, tooth, horn and shell; and even the hard, strong, hooked leg of *Eurycantha latro*, an oversize insect found in New Guinea.

Such hooks have a dimension to them that steel does not: They often float, or at least don't sink with the lifeless behavior of drawn metal, and they may exude a faint natural scent. For centuries, burbot fishermen in Sweden have sworn by hooks carved from juniper branches; the oil, they claim, attracts the fish. Such hooks are lures, not just the means by which the fish is snagged and held.

Iron, bronze and copper hooks led, in the Middle Ages, to steel–the best hooks, asserted "The Treatyse of Fysshinge wyth an Angle," in the 1496 *Boke of St. Albans*, were made from needles. (The modern versions of these two products, both relying upon high-quality wire, grew up together.) The idea of lashing feathers–as well as maybe impaling bits of food–onto a hook was already a thousand years old by then, or older. The idea of carving a representation of a baitfish to act as a lure (with a hook attached) or a decoy (to attract fish within reach of a net or spear) may be as old. Hurum's *A History of the Fish Hook* includes a sketch of a fish-shaped "lure" from the Middle Ages. It has a drilled eye at the head and a multipointed forged-iron gang hook sprouting out of its blunt tail. The first mass-produced artificial lure, however, is thought to be the British Phantom Minnow. Tackle expert Carl Luckey has traced its appearance in America back to just after 1800, and it hardly changed for more than a century afterward.

Phantom Minnows are, well, minnow-shaped. They have highly detailed metal heads with metal spinner fins attached on two sides, and two or three treble hooks, one behind the tail, the others spaced alongside the body at intervals. The tubular, tapered body is silk, usually with a forked tail and usually painted with a scale-and-spot pattern. Later in their development the fragile bodies were coated with rubber. In Britain, both Farlow's and Hardy's fishing catalogs still offered Phantom Minnows of this kind just before World War II. By then they also had developed "Ideal" Phantoms, too, with wooden bodies that undoubtedly withstood the ravages of rot and fish teeth a good deal longer, and swivels. These and the silk versions were offered in half a dozen color schemes and lengths up to four and a half inches, weighing as much as twelve drams, or three-quarters of an ounce.

The first American lure to receive a patent, in 1852, was a spinner invented by one Julio T. Buel. The most significant early American lure, however, is the Haskell Minnow, which was patented on September 20, 1859. Although the patent application specifies wood as a possible body material, the dozen or so examples known to exist at the moment are copper. They are beautifully fashioned and highly detailed, with eyes, mouth, gills, fins and tail; some have intricate scale patterns over almost the entire body, others have a simpler brushed finish. The hollow body is built on a full-length hook shank, with an eye at the front and a double hook sprouting from the tail. The rear third of the Minnow spins on this shank, and the tail fins are gracefully curved in opposite directions to make it do so. Riley Haskell, the inventor, was a gunsmith in Painesville, Ohio, and his artistic and metalworking skills are clearly superior.

The first actual Haskell Minnow I was aware of changed hands in a private sale in 1984 for a reported $800. Prompted in part by effective publicity, its value quickly spiralled upward, establishing and then breaking a number of landmark prices along the way. In the summer of 1988 another Minnow set a world-record price for antique fishing tackle by fetching $22,000 at the Richard W. Oliver Gallery auction in Kennebunk, Maine.

More than any other single item, Haskell's lure is responsible for today's antique-tackle fever. These eye-popping auction prices caught the attention of media ranging from the sporting magazines to the *New York Times* and *The Wall Street Journal*, in America and abroad. When investment collectors realized that the finest fishing tackle could be bought for prices that were still orders of magnitude less than the cost of, say, the most desirable vintage automobiles, decoys or firearms, the stampede was on. Attics and boathouses throughout America are being rifled as you read this.

REGARDLESS of the prices paid for Haskell Minnows, Comstock Flying Helgramites and a few other top-notch collectibles, the beginning collector still has a world full of diverse and interesting (sometimes even highly entertaining) lures to choose from, and at prices far less than collectable rods and reels demand.

Fishermen are generally parsimonious creatures who do not throw things away—"Never know when this might come in handy"—and who are in fact always buying more things—"*This* ought to catch ol' bucketmouth"–for the tackle box. In finest capitalistic fashion, the American entrepreneur has been feeding this urge with thousands of lures, artificial baits and assorted other fish-getters. And since you can't make an honest buck without protecting your better mousetrap from competitors, the U.S. Patent Office heard about seemingly every one of them–to its regret perhaps, for lawsuits between lure companies over design infringements became all too common in the early 1900s. As with the evolution of American fishing reels, lure history can be traced through these patent records. They outline an almost incredible family of devices whose design range from Rube Goldberg to Buckminster Fuller.

All this since the wooden-bodied plug was·born, at about the turn of this century . . . .

JAMES HEDDON, of Dowagiac, Michigan, had as much or more to do with this development as anyone. The story behind his lures has passed into American folklore, but it's an entirely credible one: Heddon, waiting for a fishing friend, was passing the time in idle whittling. Done, or maybe when the friend arrived, he tossed the wooden "plug" into the lake–whereupon a bass attacked it with enough verve to make Heddon sit up and take notice. By about 1890, he was carving purpose-made wooden fishing plugs, with hooks attached. By 1901 James Heddon and Sons was in commercial production, offering fishermen the original "wooden bait," which (when the ad copywriters got involved?) became known as the "Dowagiac Perfect Surface Casting Bait." The rest, as they say, is history, and Heddon rapidly became one of the pre-eminent names in American fishing. Heddon's most famous lure is a bulge-eyed, splay-legged, hand-carved frog with a single hook for each "foot" and a treble hook dangling from its belly–a collector's dream find, of course. The first production plugs, however, were necessarily far simpler–asymmetric torpedo shapes with angled sheet-metal collars behind the head, for splash & dash, and two or three trebles.

William Shakespeare Jr. of Kalamazoo, Michigan, got into the tackle business at the same time. He'd been granted a patent for a fishing reel in 1896, and his "Revolution" casting lure was patented early in 1901. Compared to Heddon's Dowagiac, it was quite complex, with its train of multiple spinner blades and round and/or cylindrical body parts. A well-tuned Revolution towed through the water makes enough commotion to make one think the name derived from the way everything on the lure seems to revolve busily. The maker claimed, however, that it was due to the "revolution" in fishing success that the lure brought its users. The very first Revolutions were apparently made of wood–and the patent mentions wood–but production soon switched over to aluminum. (Bauxite processing had by then been improved to the point where aluminum was no longer a semi-precious metal.)

Another grand old name, the Creek Chub Bait Company, opened its doors sometime before 1910, also in the Midwest–Garrett, Indiana. One of its first commercial products was the No.100 Wiggler, a gracefully teardrop-shaped wooden body fitted with a downward-angled metal diving lip. Creek Chub went on to pioneer natural scale finishes for lures, sometime in the late teens, which was also when the legend "CCBC" began to be stamped on the lip. The best known Creek Chub lure is probably the Pikie Minnow, which dates from around 1920; 10 years later the Jointed Pikie Minnow was introduced. (The rarest Pikie is one that most of us have never seen: the Tarpon Pikie was in the catalogs from about 1935 to the '50s; it was a simple, ultra-heavy-duty lure with a reinforced lip and only two single hooks. It wasn't the only saltwater Pikie, however, as CCBC also made a Striper version in the

'50s.) My own sentimental feelings for this lure are colored by a painful teenage memory: Some time around 1960, in an attempt to modernize my half-dozen or so "obsolete" wooden Pikie Minnows (the new ones were then plastic, almost iridescent in their shiny finishes, and would obviously catch twice as many fish), I jointed all of them by sawing them in half and adding interlocked screw eyes–thereby ruining them, by the standards of today's collector. Ouch.

The all-time most famous fishing lures, however, didn't appear until after Fred Arbogast went into the business in the late 1920s. He introduced his Hawaiian Wiggler around 1930, but that was just a warm-up. His most enduring contribution to the game was the rubber-legged "skirt" that adds such an lifelike, come-hither appeal to a plug. Arbogast's near-legendary Jitterbug then appeared toward the end of the '30s, but the idea for it was 10 years old or so by then. The story goes that he'd carved a body from a chunk of broomstick and fastened the business end of a spoon to its nose to make it dive deep. Instead it flopped crazily around on the surface, and Arbogast put it aside. Years later he came across it again, and saw it in a new light. It was a simple matter to name it after the dance craze that was sweeping the country, for the lure pops rhythmically across the water. Then Arbogast really hit his stride with the Hula Popper, introduced in 1948. Unlike the 'bug, which was first made of cedar, the Hula Popper was plastic right from the start. Collectors don't hold them in the highest regard, but to the generations of fishermen who have teased big bass to the surface with its maddening gurgle, Fred Arbogast's Hula Popper is the topwater king.

In 1980, to celebrate the 50th anniversary of its formal incorporation, the Fred Arbogast Company made a limited run of replica Jitterbugs for collectors. They were the Muskie model, made again of water-resistant cedar, and were exact copies of the original except for one detail–the hook hanger screws are longer than the originals, to make them almost impossible to pull out. Colors were natural wood, black, yellow, frog, or red-and-white, and the lures were available only by mail directly from the maker.

TODAY, however, the most widely used and the most successful freshwater lure is almost certainly the plastic worm, used primarily (but not only) for bass fishing. Just as much as Shakespeare's Revolution, it revolutionized fishing. In fact, pros early on dubbed it "the great equalizer," because with it green kids could often outfish experts equipped with conventional hard-bodied lures.

Imitation worms or eels date back at least to the mid-19th century; pork-rind versions were moderately popular in this century, and a rubber eel was patented in 1933. However, the modern synthetic version was invented in 1949 by a young Ohio machinist named Nick Creme. Again, there's a slightly folklorish story behind this particular version of the better mousetrap. Halfway through a week's fishing on Lake Houghton in Michigan, Creme ran out of nightcrawlers and he couldn't find any more to buy anywhere on the lake. Frustrated, he determined to come up with a worm that could be mass-produced and that didn't need any special care. An artificial worm, in other words.

He went home and made a lifelike steel "master" worm, which he used to produce a mold. Creme lived in Akron, the rubber city, but rubber wouldn't do as a worm material because it gave off a fish-repelling scent. But there was this new synthetic called "plastic," which had just been popularized by DuPont . . . . Creme got some from the company, and set to work on the kitchen stove to cook up a batch that would give him the right color, consistency, wiggle and smell for fishing worms. Finally he was there. He rigged the first ones up with a propeller spinner and two hooks, and went back to Lake Houghton. Success—with the fish, anyway—right from the start, and Nick Creme and his wife, Cosma, went into the business.

Success with fishermen, however, lagged behind at first. Creme says the turnaround began at the 1951 Cleveland Sports Show, when crowds gathered around his aquarium, fascinated by the lifelike wiggle of his worms. A few years later, the legend goes, his worms were suddenly being banned from certain southern fish-for-pay ponds because they caught too many expensive bass. That's just the sort of thing a fisherman needs to hear to get his acquisitive juices flowing, and there was no holding back afterward.

Today there are hundreds, perhaps thousands, of variations on Creme's original product. Plastic worms come in every imaginable size and color; they are realistically segmented and ribbed; fitted for surface or bottom work, and for every level inbetween; used in salt as well as fresh water; injected with fish-attracting flavorings; pitted to induce "sonic vibrations"; and rigged with many different spinner, hook and sinker arrangements. Finally, as well as being highly effective, they are dirt cheap and pretty durable. Some call it the perfect lure.

The collector with an eye for the future should be aware not so much of the worm, which is being produced in the millions, as of its unusual by-products. The U.S. Patent Office classifies these as "Flexible Fishing Lures," and they include imitation salamanders, insects and snakes as well as eels and worms. Some have heads, eyes, legs and feet, others have skirts, or corkscrew "twister" tails. The French-made Vivif lure, with its curved tail, that swept America in the 1960s is a good example of an oddball plastic-worm variant that may become highly collectible.

Fly-fishing gave something to the lure fisherman when hooks dressed with bucktail hair began to be put on spinners, spoons and plugs in the last century. The plastic worm returned the favor when a few innovative fly tiers realized that they too could use that material that fish seemed to like to chew on. Chief among them is John Betts, who now lives in Denver. In his search for soft-bodied flies that a trout or bass wouldn't immediately try to spit out, he developed a series of rubber and plastic imitation damselflies, beetles and other insects. Betts ties them, layer by layer, just the way classic feather-and-hair flies are made—only the materials are different. They are very effective fishing flies and they're also stunningly lifelike sculpture. Tomorrow's collectible? I think they're worth collecting right now.

BY THE 1920s, American plug-making had become an industry whose output kept the sporting press busy enthusing over the fabulous catches that were possible. Seemingly, inventive fishermen everywhere were feverishly working on their version of the better mousetrap. Factoring in the combinations and permutations that were possible with such extras as head or tail spinner or propeller blades, weedguards, hooks dressed with bucktail, joints, eyes and so on (not to mention different colors and sizes), hundreds and then perhaps thousands of plugs became available. Dizzying as these variations can be, the collector should be thankful for them. First, variety is the spice of any collection; and second, in conjunction with company records and catalog descriptions, they often help date a particular lure.

Equally important to collectors for the same reasons are the many different types of furnishings, such as eyes, hooks and swivels, and the hardware used with them, that were mere details to the fishermen who bought the lures to use. Lure authority Clyde Harbin, who signs himself as The Bassman, diagrams no less than 13 different hangers by which manufacturers fastened hooks to their lures–and that's just for starters. The Bassman also developed a complex classification and identification code by which collectors and dealers can describe lures to each other. (See his book *James Heddon's Sons Catalogs.*)

Some collectors specialize in the lures from one or more companies, designers or regions, or lures meant for particular species of fish. Even special lightweight lures to be cast with fly rods. Others concentrate on mechanical lures, with spring- or even battery-powered gadgets, such as swim fins or propellers, lights, noisemakers, or retracting hooks, built in. Then there are the collectors who hunt down only lures shaped like frogs, crawfish, mice or insects, or lures made to emit scents or blood trails. The variety is certainly there.

And who isn't beguiled at least a tiny bit by the names of some lures? Heddon offered us a Luny Frog and a Spoon-y Frog, the Zig-Wag, River Runt, Moonlight Radiant, Midget Digit, Yowser, Weedless Widow, Triple Teaser, Zaragossa Minnow and the Vamp. Creek Chub made more than Pikie Minnows and Crawdads; there was the Husky Musky, Flip-Flap, Wiggle Wizard, Ding Bat and even a Sinful Sal. The Moonlight Bait Company wanted no one to miss its message–it named its lures Bass-Eat-Us and Trout-East-Us, among other things. Pflueger took the sentimental approach with its Pal-O-Mine, but what did Brook's Baits have in mind with its 1940s-vintage "Reefers?" The Outings Co. made a Floatem Getum, and Paw-Paw the Wotta Frog–no respect for grammar there–and Kirwan a "Bad Egg." There were Hell Divers, Stump Knockers, Deep Creeps and Daily Doubles, the Goofy Gus, Staggerbugs and lots more. From the South Bend Bait Company came the famous Bass-Oreno and all the others-Orenos–Ketch, Whirl, Troll, Tarp, Babe, Surf, Midge, King, Trout, Tease, Plunk and probably more. Shakespeare got into the spirit of the thing too, with an Egyptian Wobbler, the Injun Joe, Dopey and its Little Pirate. And don't forget the lyrically named Rush Tango.

WHILE PRIME individual featherwing Atlantic salmon flies from collectible tiers such as Megan Boyd and and Ron Alcott normally sell for more than $100, the highest price known to have been paid so far for any fly is $1,900. That was for a historically significant dry fly attributed to Theodore Gordon, 1854-1915, the "father of the American dry fly." That's a far cry from the $22,000 shelled out for a Haskell Minnow, but it's nevertheless a portent of things to come. Provenance (see "Guidelines for Collectors") is considerably more difficult to establish for a fly–unlike many lures, including the Haskell, flies don't have their maker's name stamped on them. This particular fly, however, came with a letter from Gordon himself that apparently established its authenticity. A master fly dresser, like a painter, often develops a style–a way of tying knots or finishing a head, let's say–that becomes a subtle but distinctive "signature" that expert collectors and other fly tiers can "read." However, a style that can be recognized can also be mimicked, and the incentive to do so can only increase as the value of masterpiece flies appreciates.

Being made largely of feathers, fur and hair lashed down with silk thread, old flies often failed to survive the attacks of time and fish as well as have old lures made of metal and wood. However, every tackle auction and flea market can produce dozens of leather wallets and handsome japanned tin boxes crammed with old flies. It's normally impossible to attribute these to any particular fly tier, but these are usually collectible in and of themselves, as relics of earlier times. Proof–or even a strong hint–that they came from the bench of Edward Hewitt, Carrie Stevens, Roy Steenrod, Louis Rhead, Rube Cross or other famous names may lash buyers to a froth of desire, but that's rare. Since before the turn of this century, large commercial flies, such as streamers, were often sold attached to a card carrying the maker's name and other information, but these were normally detached and discarded as soon as the fly went into the buyer's fly box or wallet.

Interestingly enough, while lure collectors can easily find high-quality old goods but have fewer modern-day collectibles to choose among, collectors of flies face the opposite situation. The output of their historical heroes may have vanished, but today there are as many great fly tiers at work as there ever have been–maybe more, in fact.

All of these contemporary flies are beautifully made, and some are startlingly unusual. I've already mentioned the synthetic creations of John Betts. Californian Peter Ross, better known for his Kudo-winning fishing-tackle bags, also creates highly original and lifelike flies made of leather–many insects as well as crayfish, frogs, minnows, squid and worms. Tim England, who is a rescue paramedic with the Fort Collins, Colorado, fire department, has earned the nickname "Dr. Deerhair," for his superbly crafted and colored hair frogs, baitfish and so on. Lee Wulff, the greatest living American fly fisherman, pioneered a line of unusual plastic-bodied flies in the 1950s. These are available again, and a fortunate few have examples dressed by Wulff himself–or, even better in the eyes of traditionalists, the bushy "Wulff-type" dry flies he developed in the '30s. The vast bulk of Dave Whitlock flies are now tied under license by offshore fly factories, but the master still makes a few himself, especially as he concocts new patterns. Helen Shaw, Walt Dette, Ernest Schwiebert, Poul Jorgensen, Ted Niemeyer, Al Troth, Bob Veverka, Alcott and many other greats are still tying flies in the present too. Some of them now tie only for charity or for special orders, but a few are still full–time production tiers whose work is available and inexpensive.

Regardless of price, however, what these artisans offer the collector is instant and incontrovertible provenance of their own products.

On the hard-bodied side, there are also a few collectable lure makers who operate at the cottage-industry level. Decoy carver Russ Hofmeister, who lives in Waseca, Minnesota, is also known for his mouse lures, molded in plastic and painted by hand. He makes four sizes: Small, Medium, Large and Gigantic. Butch Lindle of Alpena, Michigan, hand-carves half a dozen lures from wood. They include two sizes of his Sucker, with rubber tails cut by hand from tire inner tubes, and the Ho-Go. He tank-tests and silk-screens them all by hand too, and numbers the first 10 of each model on the belly. Several generations from now, collectors may be hunting as feverishly for these as they are now for Jim Heddon's early frogs.

FULL-DRESS featherwing salmon flies, tied by Maxwell MacPherson, Jr. Clockwise from top left: Popham, Butcher, Torrish, Jock Scott, Baron, Green Highlander. The hackle feathers are toucan (upper) and Indian crow—themselves rare and valuable. Photograph by Charley Frieberg.

A QUILL Gordon tied by its originator, Theodore Gordon, the "father of modern American angling," approximately between 1890 and 1895. The fly is from his own personal collection, so it may have seen (light) duty on New York's Neversink. Photograph courtesy of The American Museum of Fly Fishing.

SOME FAVORITE streamer patterns: The two at upper left were tied by Charles Zibeon Southard, probably before 1940. The other three—a Yellow Tiger bucktail, at bottom; a Black Ghost, at right; and a Dot Edson— were apparently all tied by the famous Bill Edson, originator of the Edson Tiger series.

The turn-of-the-century book, Paddle & Portage, was written by Thomas Sedgwick Steele. Don Gray photograph courtesy of the American Museum of Fly Fishing.

THE HOSMER MECHANICAL FROGGIE

IT FLOATS   IT GETS 'EM

IT'S WEEDLESS

INSTRUCTIONS

Oil shaft and hinge joints with three in one (3 in 1) oil before using.
When casting, in reeling in Froggie allow a moment's hesitation between each turn of reel.
When trolling, place a buckshot sinker on the bend of each body hook. Allow time for
Froggie to reach bottom, then with the boat moving slowly, give short jerks of the rod from
horizontal to perpendicular positions. Then return rod to original position and repeat.
The nearer you have the Froggie act like a wounded live frog the bigger and more fish you
will catch.

Patent Pending

J. D. HOSMER COMPANY, 6052 Kenilworth Ave., Dearborn, Mich.

TO SAMPLE ROOM DEPT. 19   150

Remarks: Exhibit in Brown —
Schipp patent suit
Exds.—American Fox
Exds.—Lansing 1/4/31

RECEIVED DEPT. 19
BY   DATE
O8   9/16/30

DATE ARTICLE REC'D
Witnessed by   Date

THIS TICKET
ISSUED BY   O8

PATENT
NO.   —

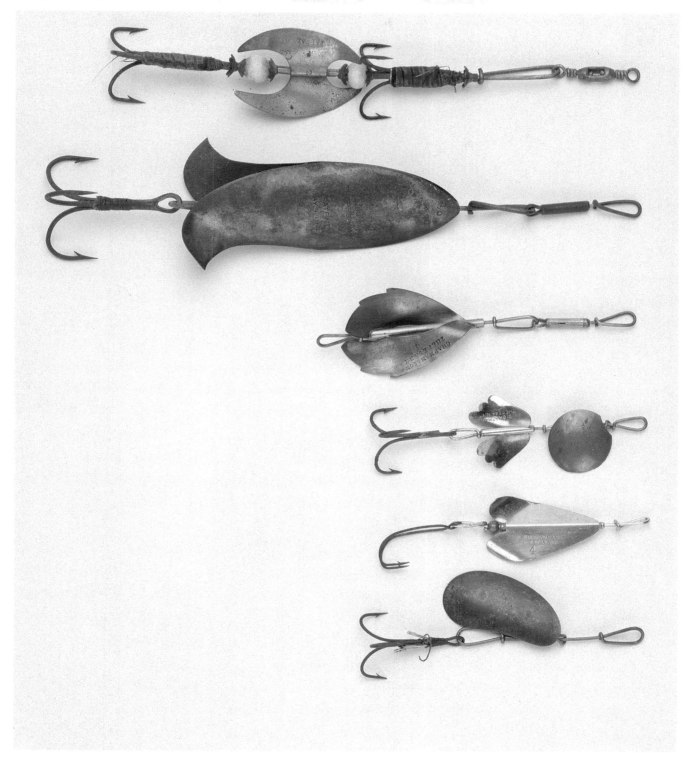

AN INTERESTING assortment of spinners. At top is a John Pepper Jr. metal lure marked "PAT. May 2, '93". The others are all stamped "W.D. Chapman, Theresa, N.Y." or "Chapman and Son".

Top to bottom: A hollow brass muskie-size lure with the patent date May 4, 1870; the body is four inches • Double-leaf spinner, probably silver-plated originally, also marked "ALLURE 1" • A tandem-spinner lure, with copper and nickel-plated leaves • An unusual double-hook arrow-head spinner • An-other unusual Chapman, with a kidney-shaped spinner and a treble hook.

THIS FIVE-INCH wooden Hosmer Mechanical Froggie lure (top) resembles a marionette, with six hinges and all the screws and springs to go along with them. The legs were meant to kick vigorously during the retrieve. This example is one of four known, in its original box, and is the only one in this yellow frog finish. It has glass eyes and three weedless hooks (two are in the belly), and was found in the rafters of what had been Hosmer's own house.

The colorful metal-body Pflueger May Bug is unfished and original, still accompanied by its factory Sample Room tag, which indicates the lure led an exciting life—appearing as some form of evidence in at least two design-infringement actions between competing manufacturers.

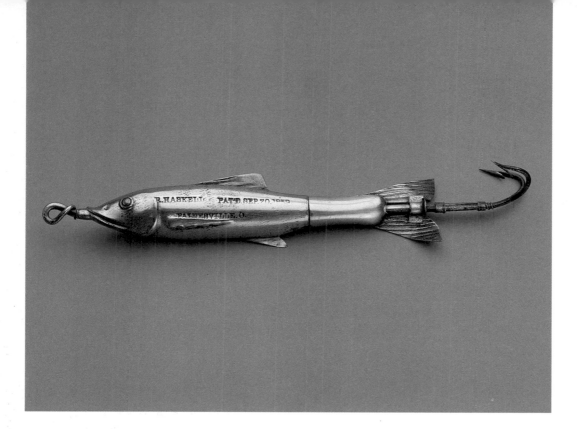

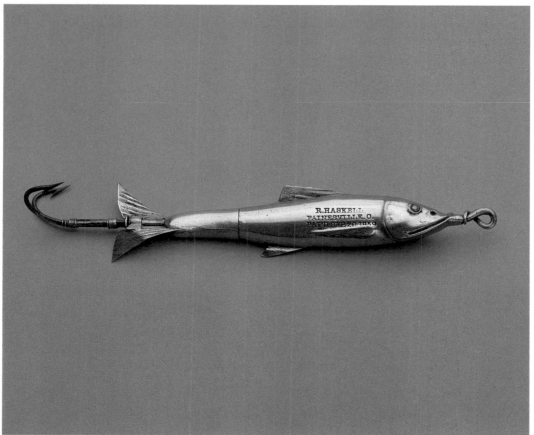

TWO VIEWS: A good example of the world's most valuable lure—the famous handmade Haskell Minnow. This smooth-finish version (Haskell also made them with delicate scale-pattern finishes; several survive) is 3 3/8 inches long overall. The revolving tail section is weighted with lead, while the head is cork-filled. About a dozen Minnows had come to light as this was written, including at least two pike-size models about 6 inches long. This one is thought to be an early version because of the unusual and perhaps experimental dual markings (the right-side version became standard). Despite the fact that it had been polished, and so is not completely original, this lure sold at the RWO Auction in Kennebunk, Maine, in July 1988 for $22,000—a record for fishing tackle.

THIS ALUMINUM box, found on an overcrowded display table at a flea market, turned out to be full of classic Atlantic salmon flies.

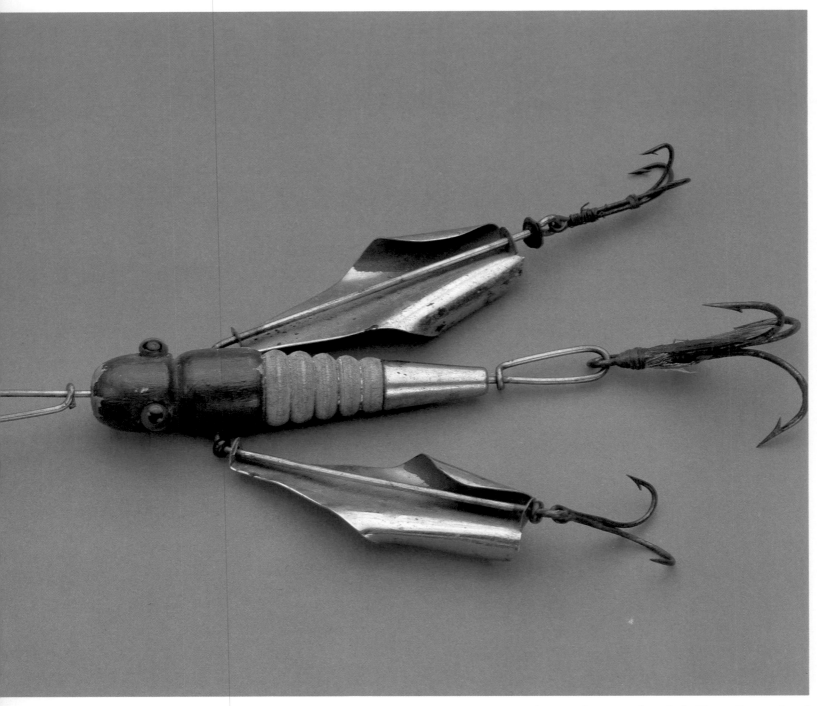

THE COMSTOCK Flying Helgramite, for which Harry Comstock, of Fulton, New York, was awarded a patent on January 30, 1883. With its turned wooden body, glass eyes and sheet-metal wings, it was one of the first American lures in commercial production. (It also must have been a nightmare to cast.) Actual length is about four inches.

HANDCARVED AND painted wooden lures by Wisconsin folk artist Pop Dean. The large double-jointed "Master Bait" muskie lure is ten inches long. The six-inch "Baby Master" brook trout is thought to be the only one made; the Bullfrog muskie lure, with its leather feet, is presently recognized as one of only three known. Both fish—which are more in the style of spearing decoys than lures—have glass eyes.

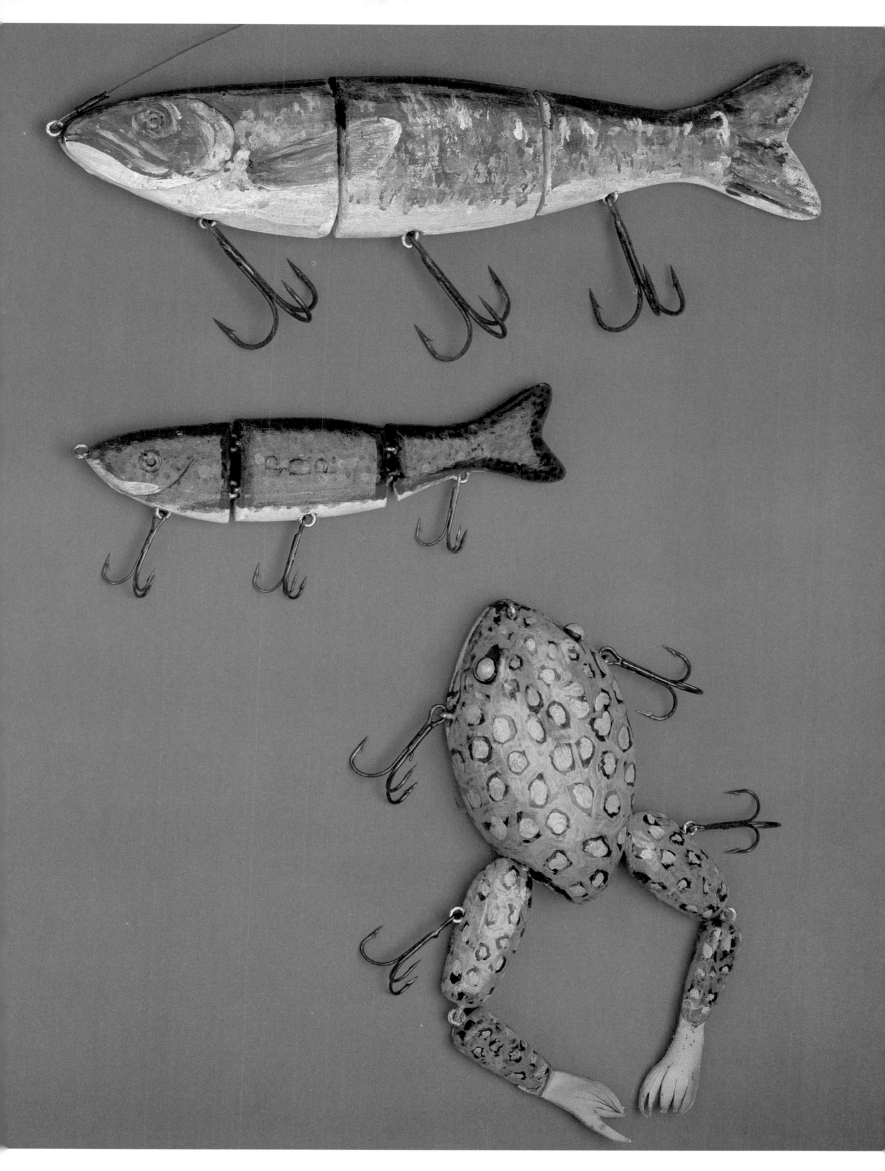

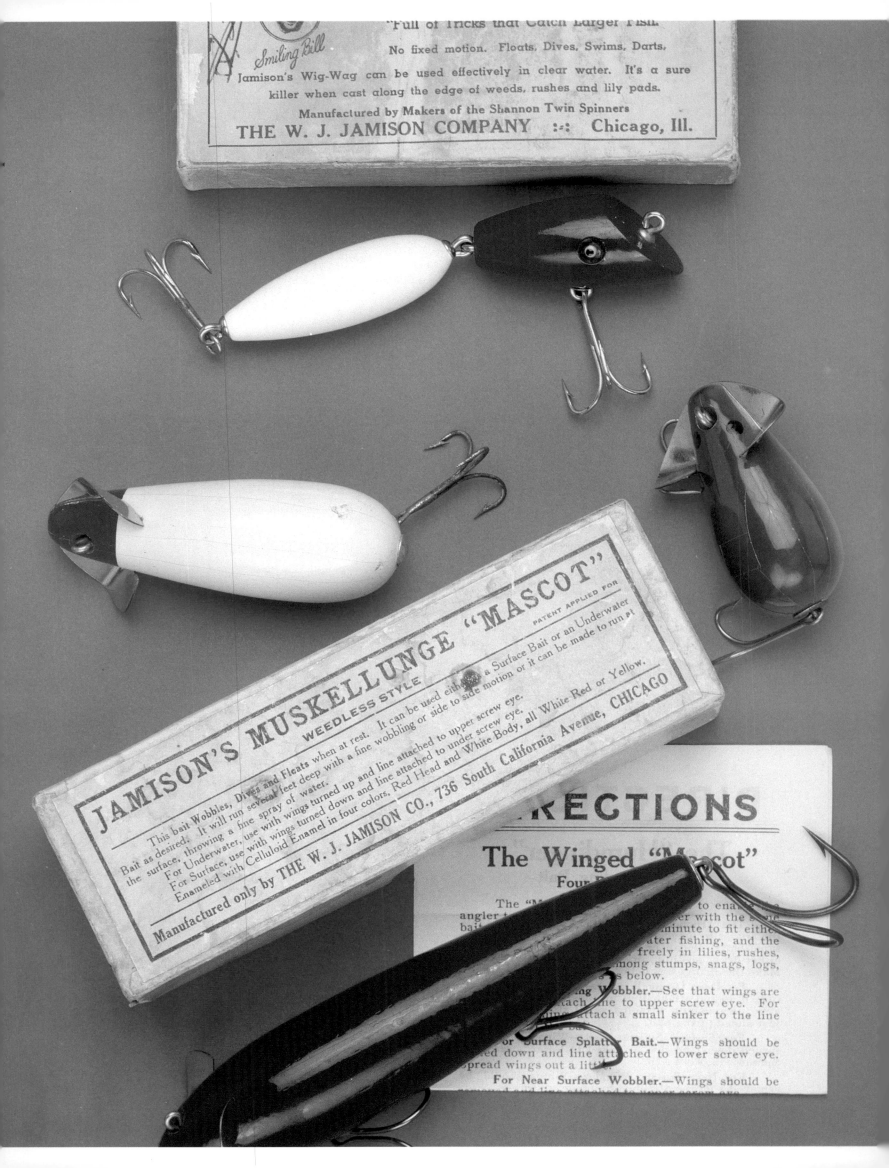

JAMISON'S MUSKELLUNGE "MASCOT"

WEEDLESS STYLE

PATENT APPLIED FOR

This bait Wobbles, Dives and Floats when at rest. It can be used either as a Surface Bait or an Underwater Bait as desired. It will run several feet deep with a fine wobbling or side to side motion or it can be made to run at the surface, throwing a fine spray of water.

For Underwater, use with wings turned up and line attached to upper screw eye.

For Surface, use with wings turned down and line attached to under screw eye.

Enameled with Celluloid Enamel in four colors, Red Head and White Body, all White Red or Yellow.

Manufactured only by THE W. J. JAMISON CO., 736 South California Avenue, CHICAGO

RECTIONS

The Winged "Mascot"

Four P...

The "M..... to enab... angler t...... er with the s.... bai......minute to fit eith...... ....ater fishing, and the ..... freely in lilies, rushes, ... among stumps, snags, logs, ... s below.

.....ng Wobbler.—See that wings are .....ttach line to upper screw eye. For .....ing..attach a small sinker to the line

..... or Surface Splatter Bait.—Wings should be .....ed down and line attached to lower screw eye. .....pread wings out a little.

For Near Surface Wobbler.—Wings should be

TOP: "THE COAXER TROUT FLY," *made by the W.J. Jamison Company and advertised by Abercrombie & Fitch in 1909. Below is a pair of Jamison Wigglers, 1 3/4 inches long. Photograph by Clyde A. Harbin, Sr.*

CHICAGO'S W.J. JAMISON COMPANY, *active from 1904 to about WWII, is best known for its metal spoons and spinners. It did, however, produce plugs too. From top: Jamison's muskie-size Wig-Wag, with original box • A green Struggling Mouse • Humdinger • A 5 1/2-inch Mascot with original box.*

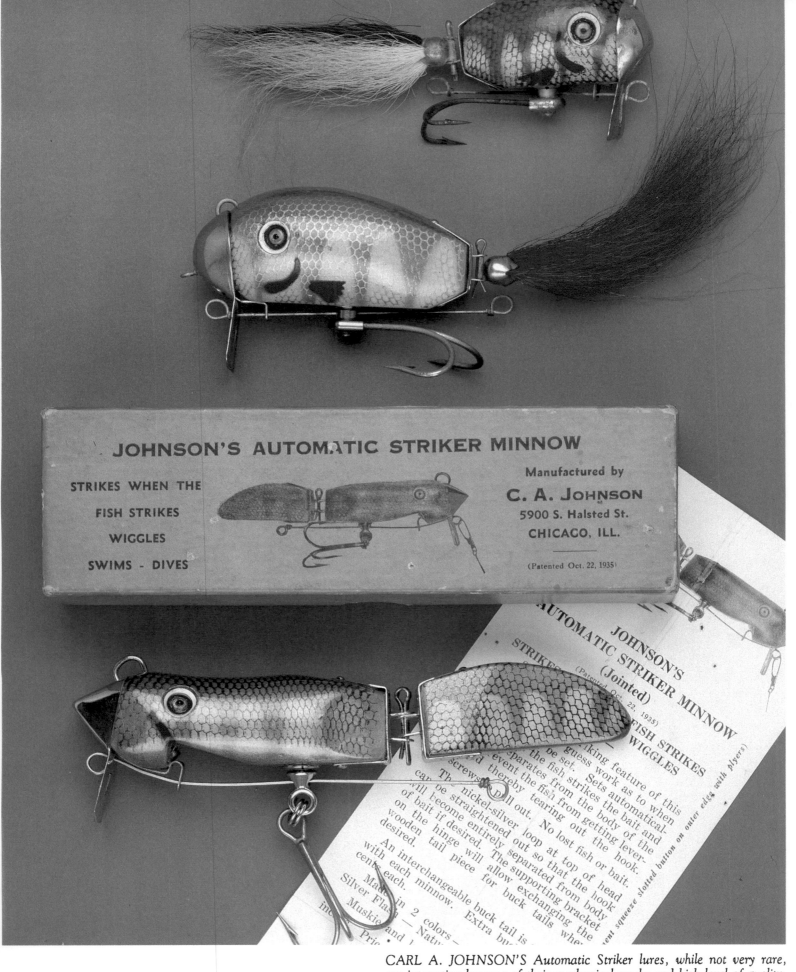

CARL A. JOHNSON'S *Automatic Striker* lures, *while not very rare, are interesting because of their mechanical works and high level of quality. The top two examples are small and large (measuring two and three inches) Automatic Striker Minnows. The bottom lure, new in its box and dating from about 1935, is the relatively rare jointed muskie Striker. The eyelet plug in the bottom of each lure was made to pop out of its socket on the strike, freeing the hook to slide down the eyelet wire; this was supposed to hold the fish more reliably.*

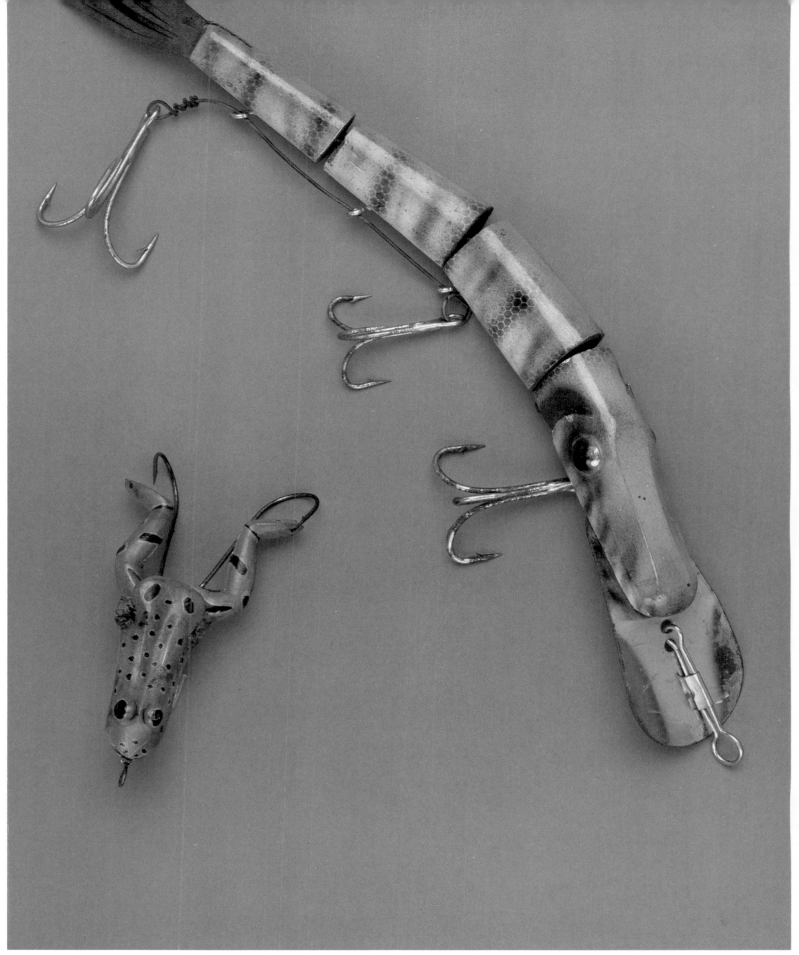

A PAIR of antique pike and bass getters. The Rhodes Mechanical Swimming Frog, which dates from about 1910, boasts glass eyes set into a flexible rubber body; the legs should stand farther away from the body, to kick backwards with each tug of the line. The eleven-inch triple-jointed muskie plug was made around 1950 by the Stewart Tackle Company, of Flint, Michigan.

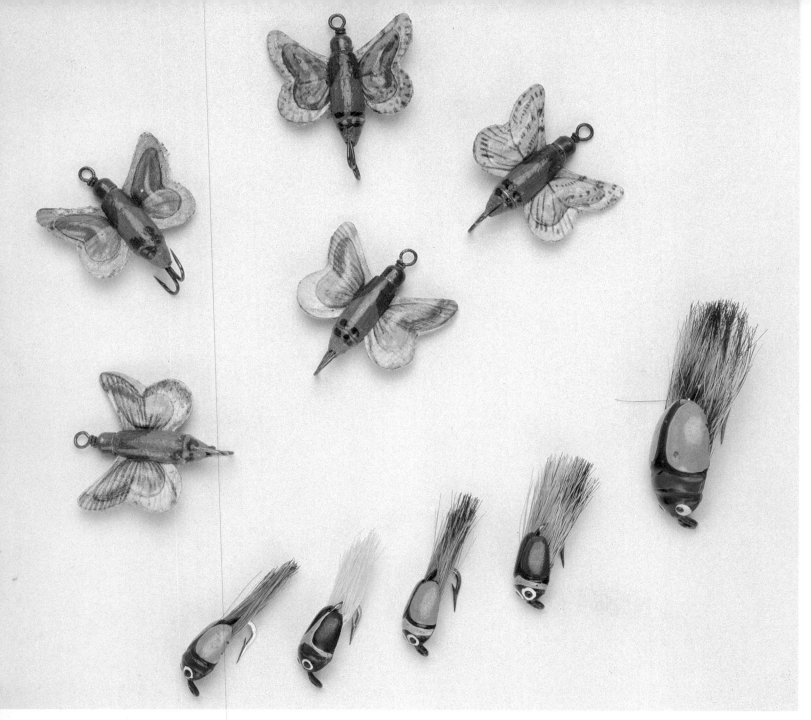

THESE RARE *fly rod lures, probably from the 1930s, are Colorado Floating Moths, with 3/4-inch bodies and hollow celluloid wings, and hand-painted tin-body beetles.*

THE TWO *spinner bodies at right are, top, a historically important J.T. Buel Patent 1852 arrowhead style, also marked "J. Warrin—NY Sole Maker, 3." Julio Buel is thought to have invented the spoon lure some time before 1848, and this is the earliest patented American lure. No one knows whether the center wire is missing or, given its age, this was originally used on a gut leader. The spiral-fin spinner body, two inches long, bears the name T.H. BATES and a patent date of June 12, 1855. It is hollow brass, with one side silver-plated.*

The larger lures, from top: A spring-loaded fish-shaped spinner type marked "L.S. Hill, Gd. Rapids, Mich, Pat. May 23, 76, Feb. 4, 79 - 2 1/2" • A rare "Buel, Whitehall, NY, 3/0" muskie or saltwater lure with a four-inch hollow German-silver body • A silver-plated spiral-fin lure stamped "Telford's Patent No.3" • A John Dineen hollow-body Spinning Metal Minnow, c. 1911.

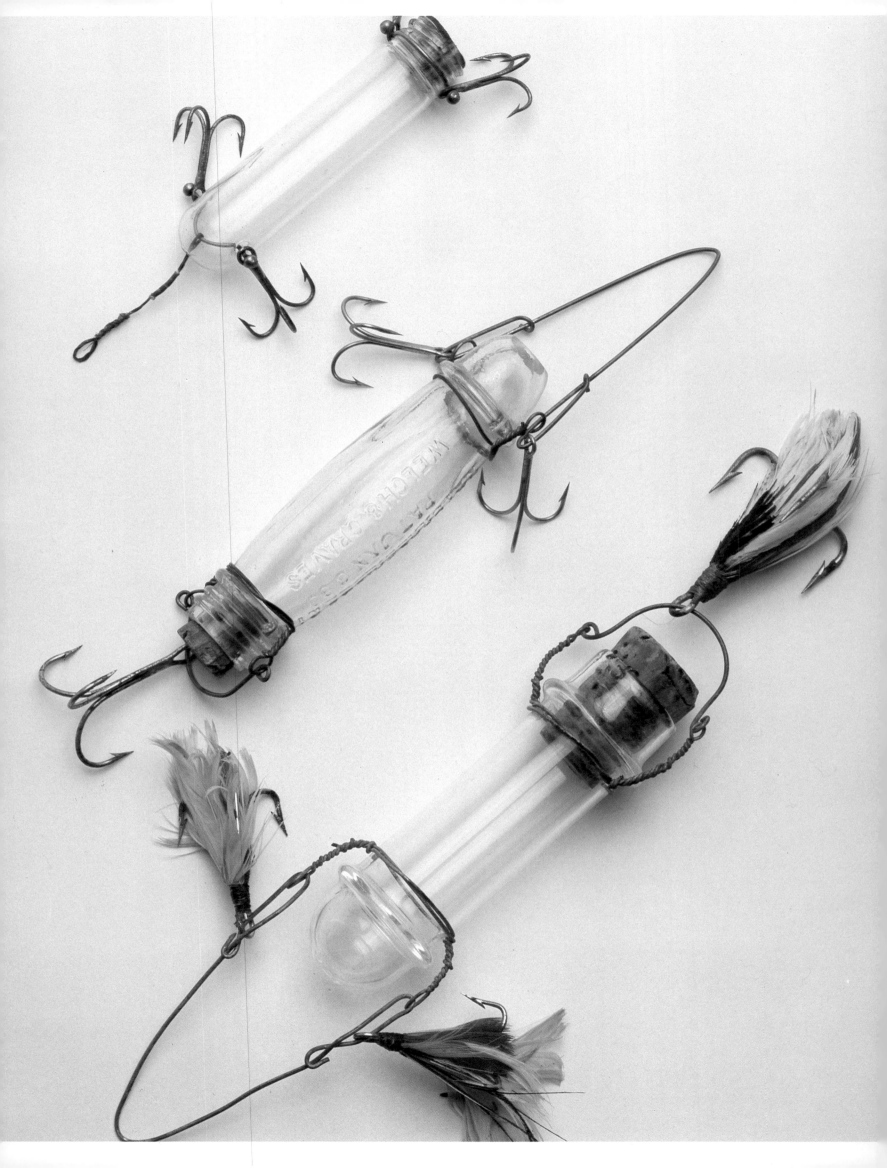

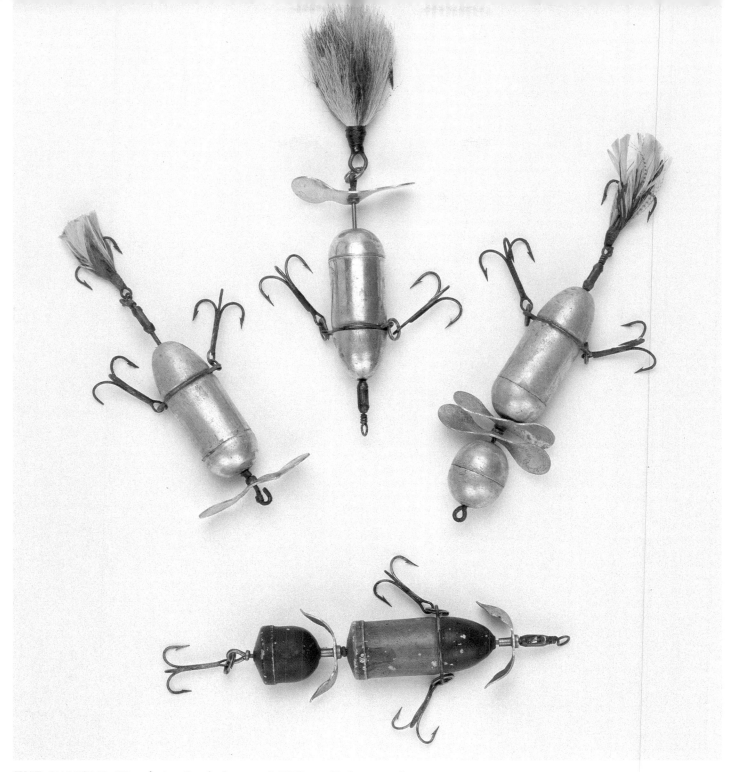

THE FAMOUS "Revolution," which earned William Shakespeare his first lure patent, February 5, 1901. The red-headed model, with its yellow body and notched props, is not a very early wooden version; it is painted aluminum. Of the three unpainted lures, the one on the right is an unusual double-spinner Revolution with reversed hooks and a dressed hook. The other two are Shakespeare-Worden Bucktail Spinners, without heads. All are about four inches overall. Shakespeare offered many different combinations of head and body shapes, propeller styles and placements, and hook attachments.

GLASS TUBE lures, probably from about 1915. As collector's oddities, these are hard to beat. From top: A relatively small (3 1/4-inch tube) Detroit Glass Minnow Tube with a twisted wire eye • A rare version with "Welch & Graves, Natural Bridge, NY, Pat Jan 3, '93" molded into the glass • A large (4 1/4-inch body) glass tube lure, with its feathered trebles still intact.

The fisherman was to slip a live minnow into the tube, which was perforated to let fresh water flow through it. The combination of the glass and the water inside was supposed to act like a lens, magnifying the size of the trapped baitfish. These examples have cork stoppers; others had screw-on metal caps.

SHAKESPEARE BLACK bass plug display. This is the only one known to exist, although one or two others may have been made. It was found in its original wooden shipping crate, with two factory labels and a shipping label dated April 6, 1934. The fish are life-size plaster casts. The lures are wooden Shakespeare Swimming Mice, which although they were not found on the board are of the right vintage.

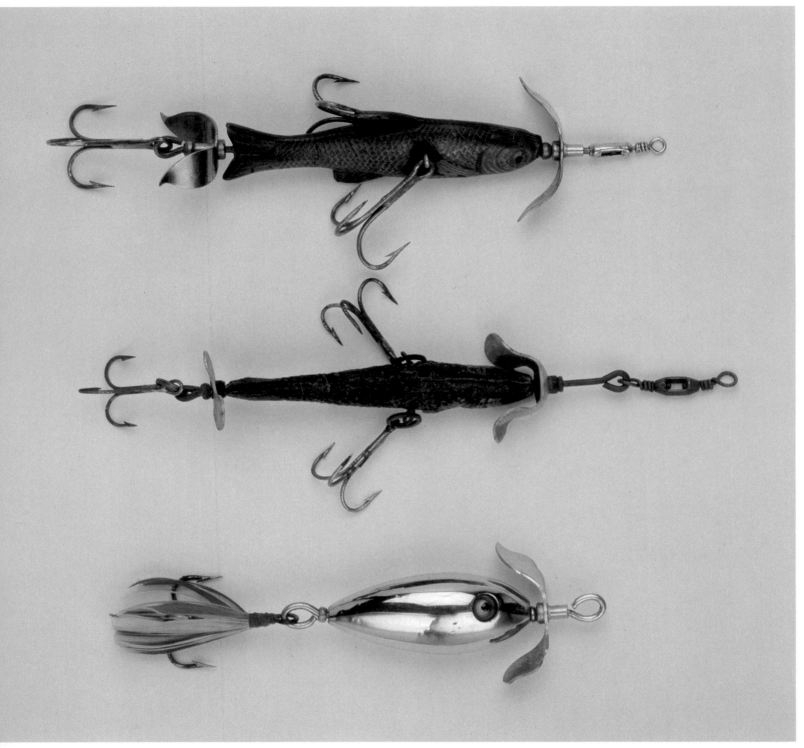

SHAKESPEARE MINNOWS. *The two rubber versions are both Evolution Baits, which the company sold for more than 30 years, beginning in about 1902. The top lure, with the curved propeller, dates from about 1912. The other is a rare early model marked "Pat. Applied For."*

The elegant 1 7/8-inch "00 Metal Plated" Minnow was produced around 1910; it has glass eyes, a notched propeller, and—under the nickel plate—a wooden body.

PFLUEGER "NEVERFAIL" *Minnows, which were made from the late 1920s well up into the '50s. The luminous gold-spotted version—new in its box, complete with instructions and the store tag—is the large size, 3 5/8 inches, with double sets of side trebles. The other two are the smaller, three-hook models, one done in the company's green crackleback finish.*

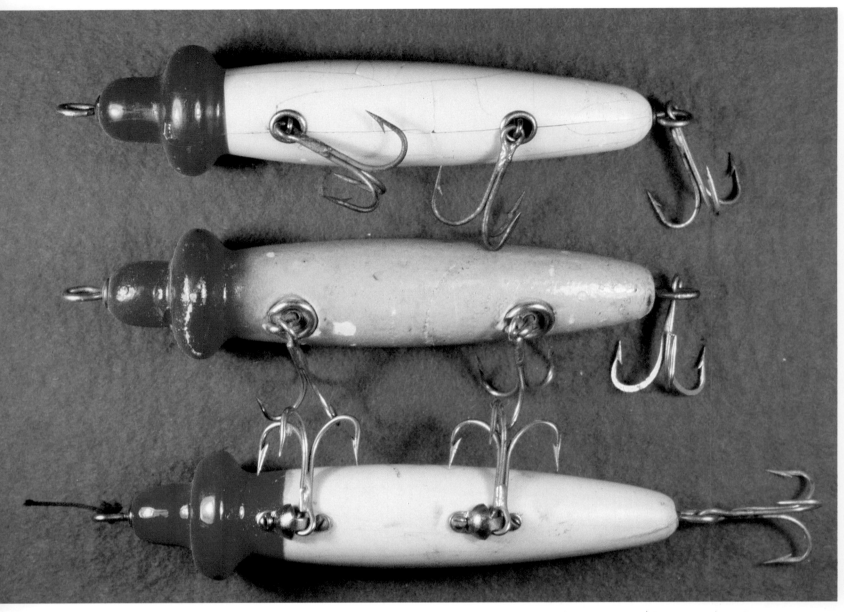

A TRIO of 3600-series Pfluegers. From the top: An early Magnet finished in the company's famous "Luminous" enamel, with concealed twisted-wire belly hook hangers • Another Magnet, this one with the 1911-vintage "Neverfail" belly hook hangers • A "Merit"—Pflueger changed the name in 1935—showing the later-style one-piece hook hangers.

Magnets are very similar to Shakespeare's Surface Wonder lure (which has its hooks mounted farther back from the head). Lure experts suspect both companies were buying blanks from the same supplier. Photograph by Clyde A. Harbin, Sr.

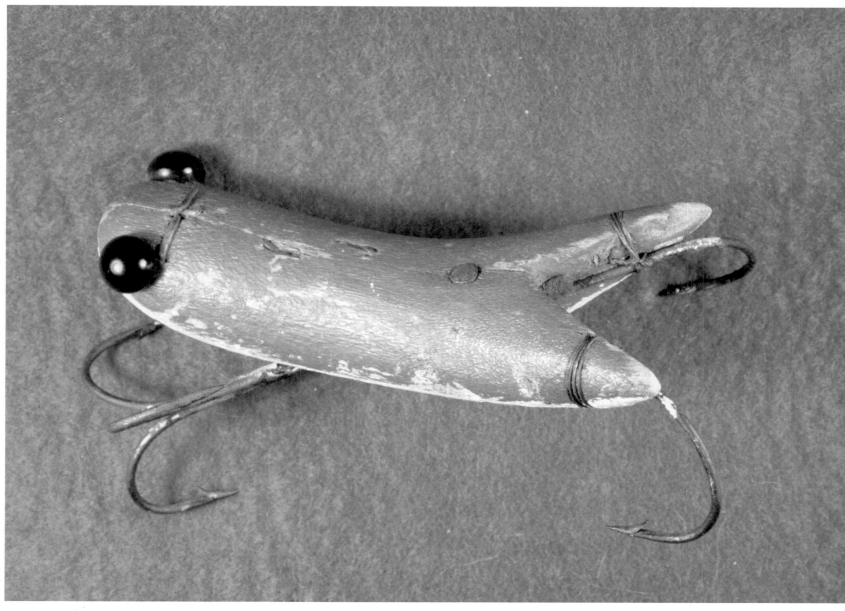

AN ULTRARARE 1898 Heddon Wooden Frog, hand-carved most likely by James Heddon himself. About a dozen proven examples have surfaced, along with a number of handmade replicas that may—or may not—be marked as such. This lure could be called the first American "plug," and it marked the founding of the Heddon tackle empire. Photograph by Clyde A. Harbin, Sr.

"DOWAGIAC" SURFACE BAIT
No. 200

No. 200 (EXPERT)

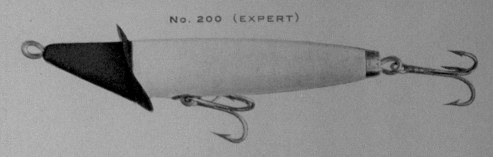

This is the old reliable "**Dowagiac**" Expert, made only in the combination of colors shown in illustration.

This is a Surface lure to be used preferably for casting, but also adaptable to "skittering" or "bobbing." It operates perfectly upon the surface of the water and avoids weeds to a considerable extent. It can be used successfully among lily-pads and rushes if properly handled and is a great attractor and practically sure killer of all of the smaller species of surface biting game fishes.

Has no spinners and is supplied with either two treble hooks only, as shown in illustration, or with two additional treble hooks on the sides. (If the four treble hook variety is wanted specify No. 2.)

Weight, approximately 12 pwts; length of body 4 1-2 ins.
Price, each, prepaid by mail, 65c.

"DOWAGIAC" SURFACE MINNOW
No. 300
No. 300 (FANCY BACK)

Shown above in Fancy Back White belly finish, is also supplied in rainbow colors, as follows:

Green Back. Pink and Yellow sides and White belly, No. 301; or blended White finish consisting of White body with Slate colored back, No. 302.
Has two spinners and one regular treble hook at the rear and a specially formed treble hook on the belly.

This is a Surface Minnow, operating successfully on all species of Surface biting game fishes. It is specially adapted for taking the large Bass of Florida and other southern states.
Weight, approximately 18 pwts; length of body 4 inches.
Price, each, prepaid by mail, 75c.

PAGE 17 of the Heddon catalog of 1910. Photograph by Clyde A. Harbin, Sr.

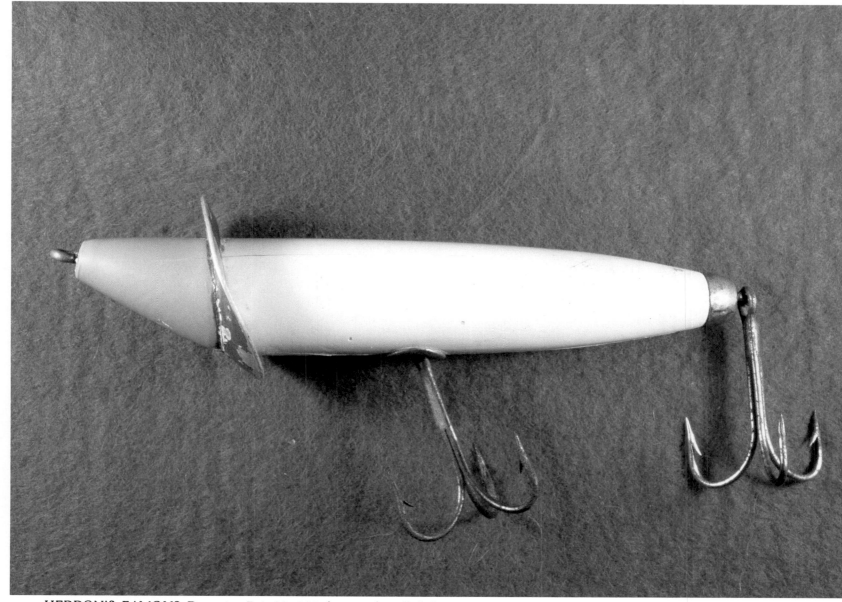

HEDDON'S FAMOUS Dowagiac Bait No.200 (commonly called the slope-nose), as seen in the company's 1906 catalog. The metal collar is held in place with one pin on the bottom, and the lure has deep brass hook cups and a brass tail cap. Photograph by Clyde A. Harbin, Sr.

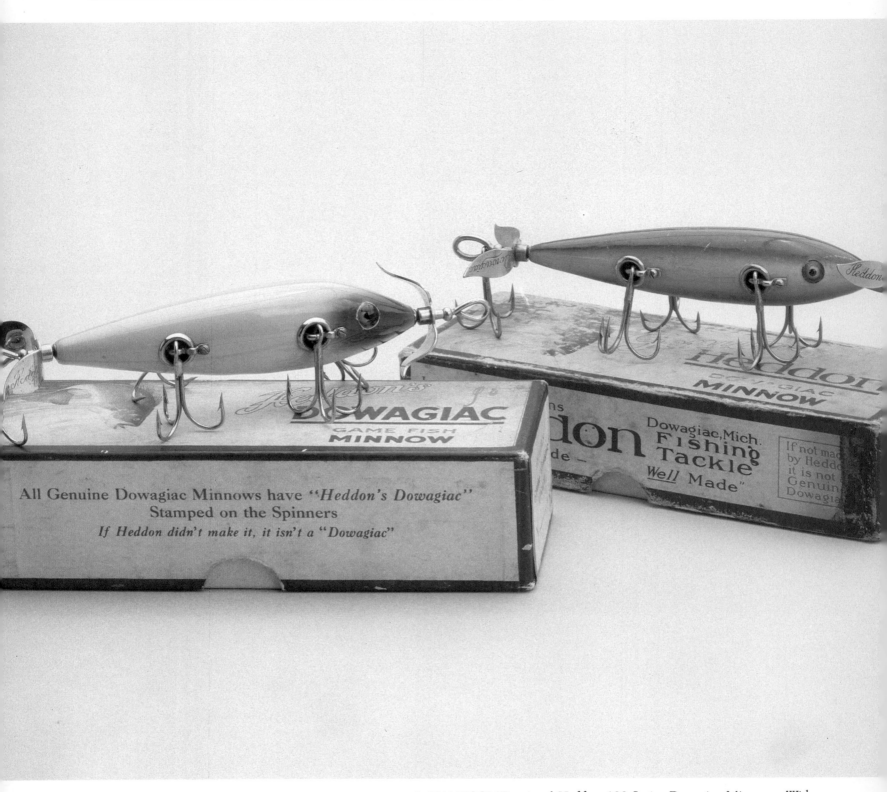

A HANDSOME *pair of Heddon 100-Series Dowagiac Minnows. With their cup-and-screw hook mounts and their wooden boxes, these were probably made in the teens. The 2 5/8-inch Minnow on the left is the newer of the two, because of its fatter body. The plastic hook protectors on the older 2 7/8-inch lure were added later. The Model 100 Minnow debuted in 1904 or 1905 and stayed in production until the early 1940s. Tackle experts can date Minnows by subtle evolutions in body size and shape, gill marks, hooks, and hardware.*

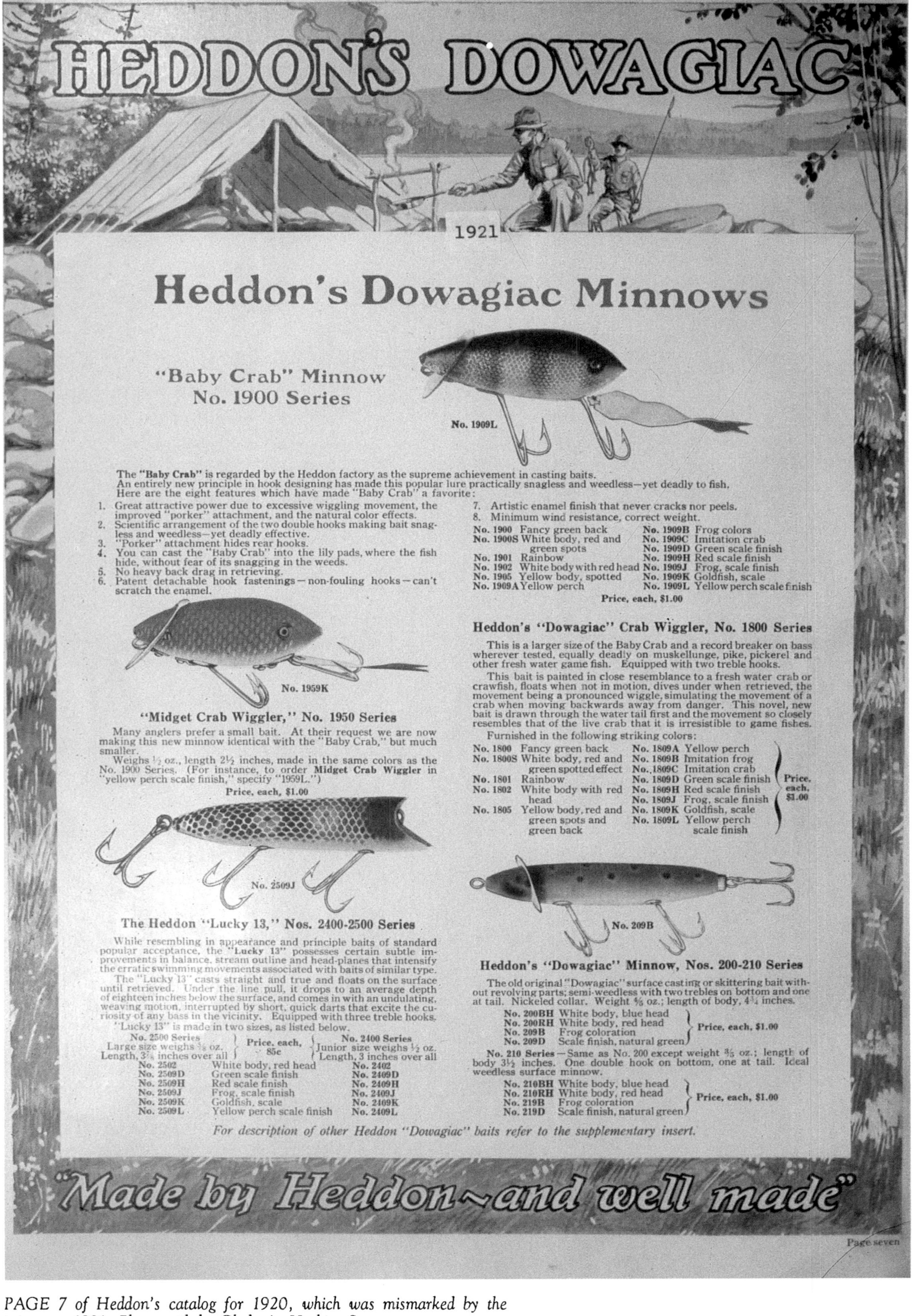

HEDDON'S DOWAGIAC

1921

Heddon's Dowagiac Minnows

"Baby Crab" Minnow No. 1900 Series

No. 1909L

The **"Baby Crab"** is regarded by the Heddon factory as the supreme achievement in casting baits.
An entirely new principle in hook designing has made this popular lure practically snagless and weedless—yet deadly to fish.
Here are the eight features which have made "Baby Crab" a favorite:

1. Great attractive power due to excessive wiggling movement, the improved "porker" attachment, and the natural color effects.
2. Scientific arrangement of the two double hooks making bait snagless and weedless—yet deadly effective.
3. "Porker" attachment hides rear hooks.
4. You can cast the "Baby Crab" into the lily pads, where the fish hide, without fear of its snagging in the weeds.
5. No heavy back drag in retrieving.
6. Patent detachable hook fastenings—non-fouling hooks—can't scratch the enamel.
7. Artistic enamel finish that never cracks nor peels.
8. Minimum wind resistance, correct weight.

No. 1900	Fancy green back	**No. 1909B**	Frog colors
No. 1900S	White body, red and green spots	**No. 1909C**	Imitation crab
		No. 1909D	Green scale finish
No. 1901	Rainbow	**No. 1909H**	Red scale finish
No. 1902	White body with red head	**No. 1909J**	Frog, scale finish
No. 1905	Yellow body, spotted	**No. 1909K**	Goldfish, scale
No. 1909A	Yellow perch	**No. 1909L**	Yellow perch scale finish

Price, each, $1.00

No. 1959K

"Midget Crab Wiggler," No. 1950 Series

Many anglers prefer a small bait. At their request we are now making this new minnow identical with the "Baby Crab," but much smaller.

Weighs ½ oz., length 2½ inches, made in the same colors as the No. 1900 Series. (For instance, to order **Midget Crab Wiggler** in "yellow perch scale finish," specify "1959L.")

Price, each, $1.00

Heddon's "Dowagiac" Crab Wiggler, No. 1800 Series

This is a larger size of the Baby Crab and a record breaker on bass wherever tested, equally deadly on muskellunge, pike, pickerel and other fresh water game fish. Equipped with two treble hooks.

This bait is painted in close resemblance to a fresh water crab or crawfish, floats when not in motion, dives under when retrieved, the movement being a pronounced wiggle, simulating the movement of a crab when moving backwards away from danger. This novel, new bait is drawn through the water tail first and the movement so closely resembles that of the live crab that it is irresistible to game fishes.

Furnished in the following striking colors:

No. 1800	Fancy green back	**No. 1809A**	Yellow perch
No. 1800S	White body, red and green spotted effect	**No. 1809B**	Imitation frog
		No. 1809C	Imitation crab
No. 1801	Rainbow	**No. 1809D**	Green scale finish
No. 1802	White body with red head	**No. 1809H**	Red scale finish
		No. 1809J	Frog, scale finish
No. 1805	Yellow body, red and green spots and green back	**No. 1809K**	Goldfish, scale
		No. 1809L	Yellow perch scale finish

Price, each, $1.00

No. 2509J

The Heddon "Lucky 13," Nos. 2400-2500 Series

While resembling in appearance and principle baits of standard popular acceptance, the **"Lucky 13"** possesses certain subtle improvements in balance, stream outline and head-planes that intensify the erratic swimming movements associated with baits of similar type.

The "Lucky 13" casts straight and true and floats on the surface until retrieved. Under the line pull, it drops to an average depth of eighteen inches below the surface, and comes in with an undulating, weaving motion, interrupted by short, quick darts that excite the curiosity of any bass in the vicinity. Equipped with three treble hooks.

"Lucky 13" is made in two sizes, as listed below.

No. 2500 Series — Large size weighs ⅝ oz. Length, 3⅝ inches over all — **Price, each, 85c** — **No. 2400 Series** — Junior size weighs ½ oz. Length, 3 inches over all

No. 2500 Series		No. 2400 Series
No. 2502	White body, red head	**No. 2402**
No. 2509D	Green scale finish	**No. 2409D**
No. 2509H	Red scale finish	**No. 2409H**
No. 2509J	Frog, scale finish	**No. 2409J**
No. 2509K	Goldfish, scale	**No. 2409K**
No. 2509L	Yellow perch scale finish	**No. 2409L**

No. 209B

Heddon's "Dowagiac" Minnow, Nos. 200-210 Series

The old original "Dowagiac" surface casting or skittering bait without revolving parts; semi-weedless with two trebles on bottom and one at tail. Nickeled collar. Weight ⅘ oz.; length of body, 4¼ inches.

No. 200BH	White body, blue head	**Price, each, $1.00**
No. 200RH	White body, red head	
No. 209B	Frog coloration	
No. 209D	Scale finish, natural green	

No. 210 Series—Same as No. 200 except weight ⅗ oz.; length of body 3½ inches. One double hook on bottom, one at tail. Ideal weedless surface minnow.

No. 210BH	White body, blue head	**Price, each, $1.00**
No. 210RH	White body, red head	
No. 219B	Frog coloration	
No. 219D	Scale finish, natural green	

For description of other Heddon "Dowagiac" baits refer to the supplementary insert.

"Made by Heddon~and well made"

Page seven

PAGE 7 of Heddon's catalog for 1920, which was mismarked by the printer as 1921. Photograph by Clyde A. Harbin, Sr.

THE HEDDON 150 Series were larger Minnows with two sets of side trebles. Both of these are 3 3/4 inches and have the distinctive L-shaped hook hangers. The 150s were manufactured, always in wood, until the early 1950s, and then reissued—in wood again—in 1973 as part of Heddon's Classic Series.

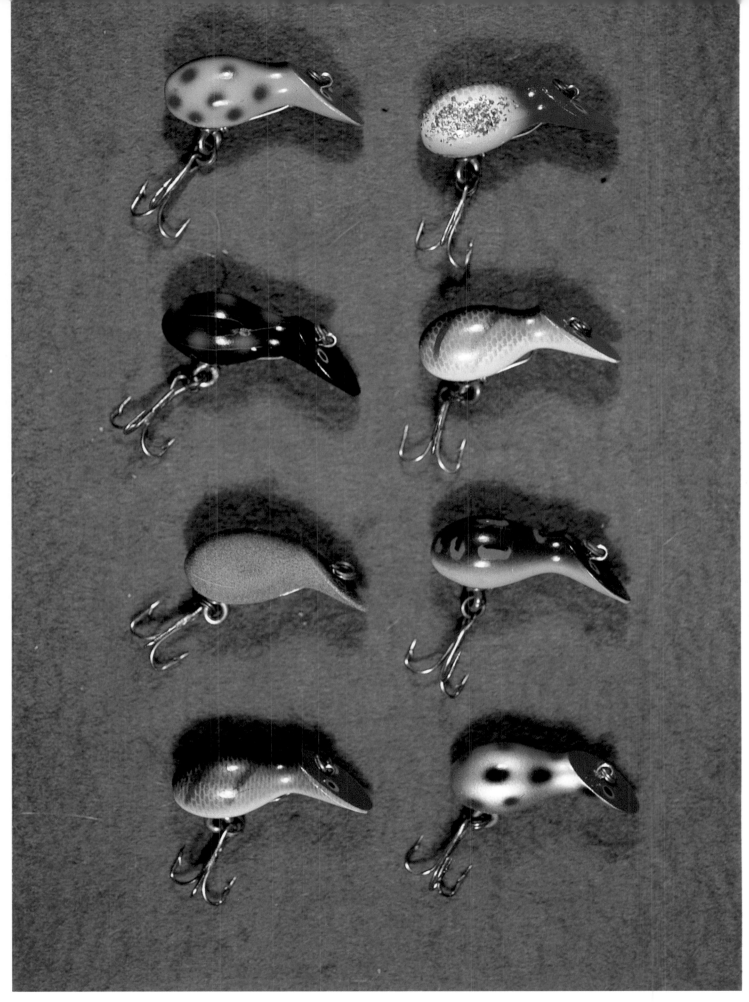

A LINEUP of new Heddon 300-Series Widgets, 1 1/4 inches long, from the early 1950s. Factory colors, clockwise from top right: Spotted Orange, Black with orange spots, Grey Mouse, Yellow Perch Scale, Silver Body with Red & Black Spots, Bull Frog, Yellow Perch Scale, Red Head Flitter. Photograph by Clyde A. Harbin, Sr.

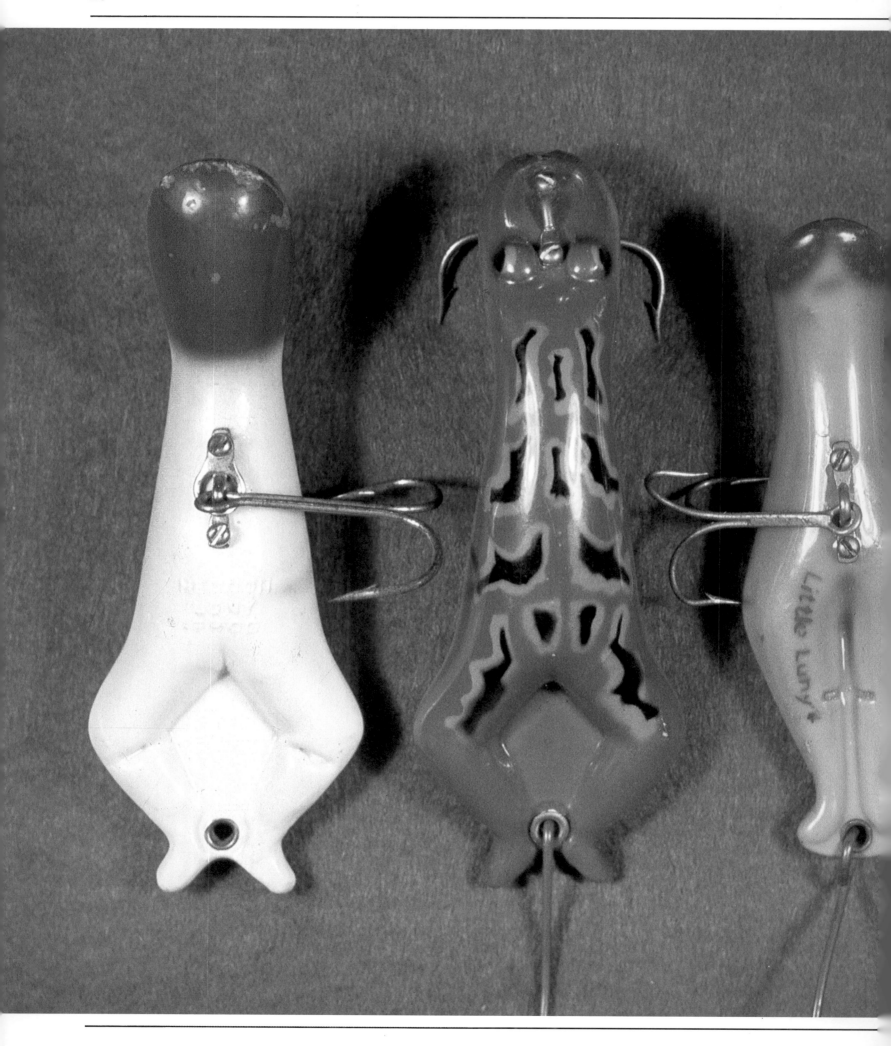

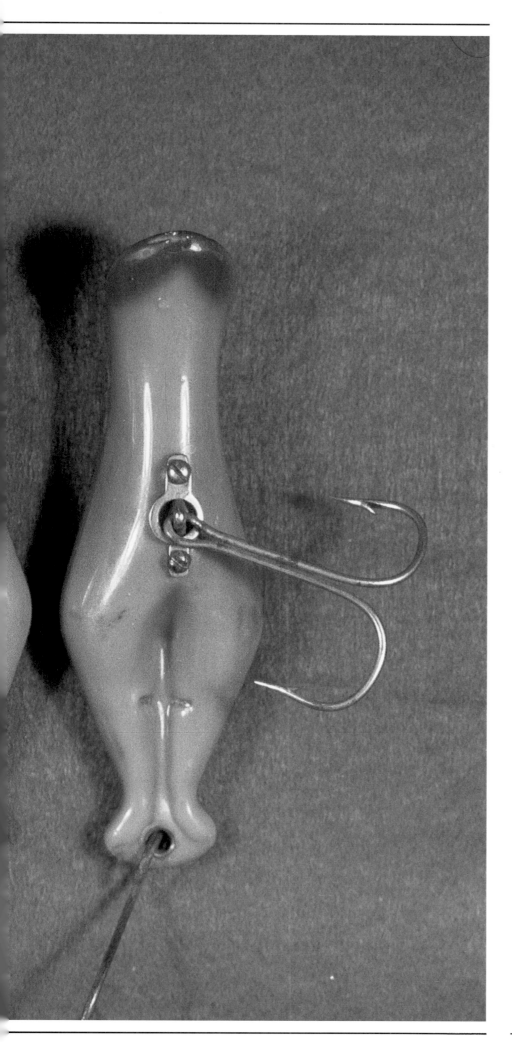

HEDDON LUNY Frogs. Left to right: A red-head No. 3500, the rarest • A Web Foot Luny Frog, in the relatively scarce closed-leg style • A pair of Heddon's #3400 Little Luny Frogs; the one on the end has the so-called toilet-seat hook hangers, one of the features that collectors date lures by. Luny Frogs were made of Pyralin, which proved too fragile. Photo by Clyde A. Harbin. Sr.

BETWEEN-THE-WARS Heddons: Next to the two River-Runtie-Spooks is a Punkie-Spook. Below, right to left: A pair of Pop-Eye Frogs and a small Wilder-Dilg Spook. Photograph by Clyde A. Harbin, Sr.

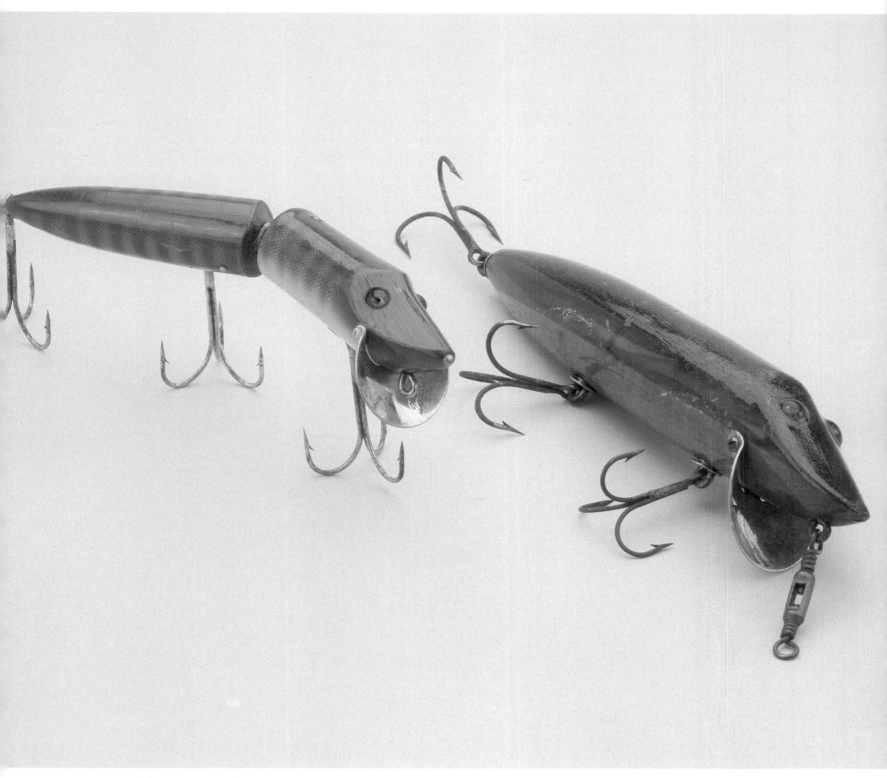

ON THE left is a seven-inch Heddon Giant Jointed Vamp, in pike scale finish, probably made in the late '30s. Alongside is a superb and unusual Heddon Musky Vamp, made of layers of walnut, cedar, and birch with a clear finish. It may not have been a regular production model.

A JAMES Heddon's Sons No. 10 "Brann's Glory" Wilder-Dilg feathered lure, with original box. Photograph by Clyde A. Harbin, Sr.

BOTH THESE Creek Chub Bait Company frogs are floating plugs, with upward-pointing single hooks to let them slide over lily pads and vegetation. The Wee Dee, left, was part of the lineup for about a decade, from 1936 on; all three hooks could pivot up and down, to be weedless. Forerunner of the Wee Dee was the Weed Bug Frog, right, which had glass eyes and wire weed guards. Catalog illustrations show Weed Bugs with long wire leaders attached.

A MODERN display board, this one belonging to a tackle dealer who has set up at a flea market. These plugs range from medium-old to undistinguished—but for someone looking to start up, for example, a Creek Chub collection, it would be a fine place to begin.

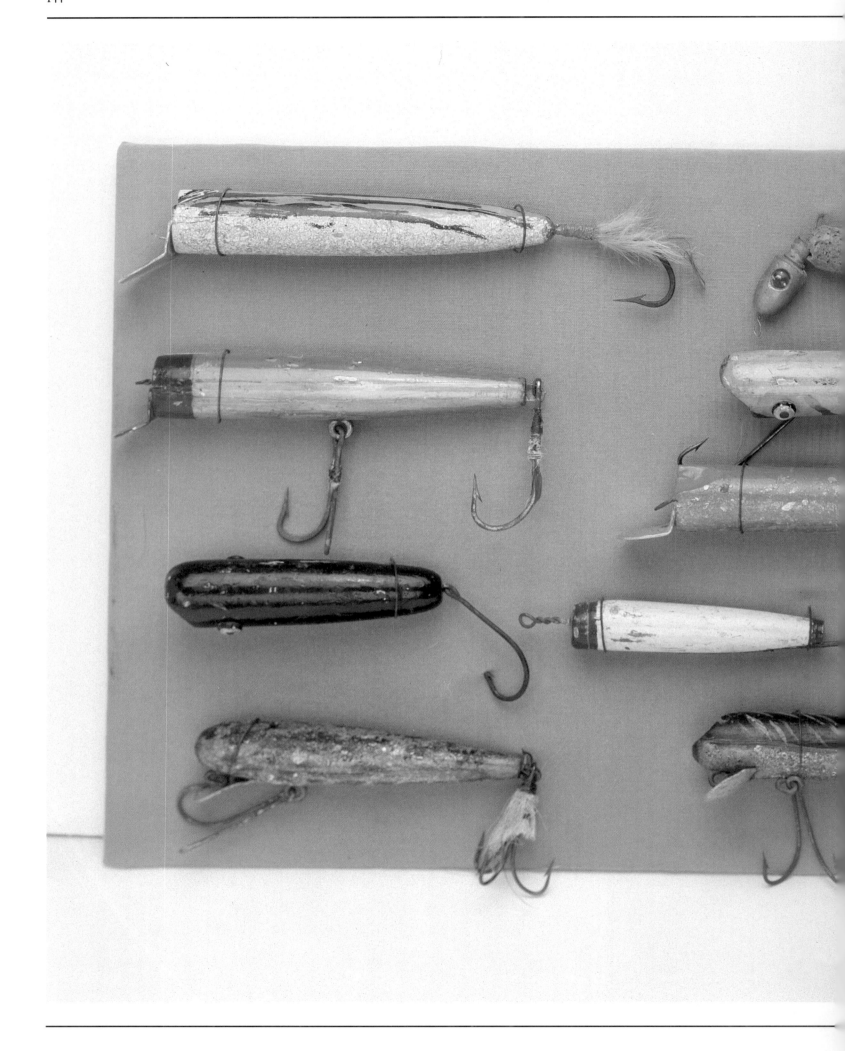

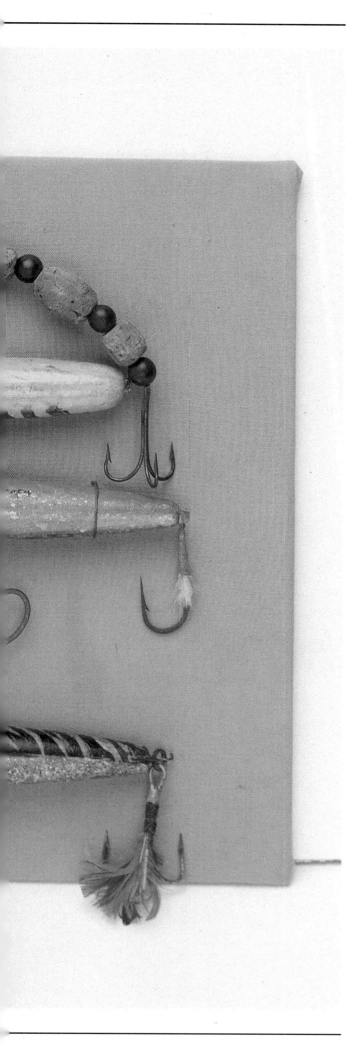

ANOTHER DISPLAY board, this one loaded with "Captain Gooch"-type striped-bass lures. The name came from the first of these plugs, reputedly carved from the mahogany legs of Capt. Gooch's table, in Sandy Hook, Long Island. The box this fits in is signed "Made by S. Schultz, Brooklyn, NY, 1940-1956."

A PAIR of classic (but recent—note plastic box sleeves) 7 3/4-inch
wooden-body Creek Chub Giant Pikie Minnows, new in their boxes, and a
Baby Injured Minnow in CCBC's "Fire Plug" finish. The Baby, with its
cardboard box and flattened side, is older.

DECOYS

THE IDEA of attracting fish within reach by using a decoy seems absurd only to the waterfowl gunner. It is illogical to him. He (and it is still almost exclusively *he*; women, even those who might shoot upland birds or big game, almost universally reject being cold, wet and motionless on purpose) arranges his decoys to look as comforting as possible. He may put out dozens or even a hundred or more blocks, to convince the high fliers that food, company and safety lie here below. Waterfowlers even resort to what they call "confidence" decoys–fakes like maybe snipe or even swans–set along the edges of their duck or goose sets, to amplify the homey atmosphere.

Waterfowl, especially the migratory flocks, love companionship. It makes sense to us, in a Disney-esque way; they're warm-blooded, raise their young with devotion, and the geese are even monogamous. Higher forms of life simply behave that way (geese are particularly high life-forms, to the shore gunner). Fish? Fish are cold-blooded, lay thousands of eggs and then maybe swim away. What, says the goose hunter, can a decoy offer to a fish?

The big-game hunter would know, or the perceptive fisherman. Think of a fish decoy not as a confidence-booster. Think of it rather as the tiger hunter's tethered goat. *That* kind of a decoy. Fish, whatever their size, tend to be rapacious predators and, like the tiger, always on the lookout for an easy meal. A decoy fish, hovering in the water, perhaps "swimming" slowly back and forth, seemingly without a care, big enough to be worth eating, not so big as to be troublesome, represents just that.

We could also think of a fish decoy as essentially a lure, without a hook. We supply the hook–not far above that tempting decoy hovers a fisherman with a spear, waiting just as motionless, maybe shading his eyes to peer down into the green water. Comes a hungry pike or muskellunge, walleye, lake trout, even a sturgeon . . . .

It works. It can work so well that many states long ago outlawed the use of fish decoys. In the upper Midwest, though, their use lingered, until now only in parts of Wisconsin, Michigan and Minnesota is this form of fishing still allowed. These ice fishermen don't set out dozens of tip-ups and slide from hole to hole, looking for a waving flag. They huddle in tiny shanties or Indian-style spearing tents that keep the light out, and instead of baited hooks, they dangle their decoys. Fish decoys aren't just hung from the ice on lanyards; they're usually swum gently up and down, in a circular pattern, on their own jigging sticks. If they look to be staggering from some injury, so much the better.

Over a light-colored sandy bottom, a large fish shows up with startling clarity in the green winter water, when all ripples are quelled by the ice. Waiting above, an experienced fisherman knows how to compensate for the refraction of light in water, and drives his weighted spear, its multiple tines already in the water, downwards with strength and accuracy. It's not as easy as it may sound; cold is always a problem, exacerbated by the need to lie motionless yet alert as the hours tick by. When a fish finally appears, it has to be very close to be in range–spears must be fairly compact, and the ice itself might be two or three feet thick in a Wisconsin winter. Nor is a successful "stick" the end of the fisherman's troubles–imagine for a moment lying on your belly on the ice, attached by a pole to a hundred-pound sturgeon fighting for its life. Which one of you will drag the other through the hole?

OLD CARVED fish decoys are almost never slavish imitations, in the style of modern photo-realistic sculptures. Overall shape, size and sometimes color were more important to decoy carvers than exact renditions of, for example, tail rays or spot patterns. The idea was to catch fish, not painstakingly recreate them. However, while the gunner could often get by with duck silhouettes that just looked good from afar, fish decoys had to be able to pass inspection in all three dimensions *and* swim more or less convincingly at the same time.

Virtually all fish decoys were made with at least some fins of wood, tin, copper, wire mesh, leather or even lead, and the type could be a clue to their origin. (New York decoys often had leather tails, for example.) Most had eyes, carved in or formed with furniture tacks, nailheads, rivets, glass beads or just spots of paint. Most also have carved or painted mouths and gills. Some have, or had, extraordinary finishes–ranging from bold, bright nail polish to spangly sequins to real fish skin. These too can help identify an unknown decoy. Foodfish decoys from Michigan, for example, were typically finished in bright colors; those made in upstate New York, on the other hand, are generally far more subdued-looking.

All "real," i.e. authentic working, decoys also have, or had at one time, hangers to attach the lanyard line. These ranged from a single screw-eye or wire staple to rows of same, or a row of holes punched in a hanger bracket, which on fancier decoys might be shaped like a dorsal fin. Different hanger holes let the fisherman adjust his decoy's balance, to swim level or slightly head-up in the water. Bending the sheetmetal fins or tail also affected its swimming style, stabilizing it or making it flutter or wobble as though injured. This tuning is as important to a decoy as it is with a diving lure (and so is the skill of the "operator").

Decoys by definition have no hooks attached, which is not to say no one ever tried it. However, even when decoys were still legal throughout New England and the upper Midwest, hooked decoys reputedly were not. In some areas they were known as cheaters.

Being normally (but not always) made of wood such as pine, basswood or cedar, spearing decoys would not sink without some added weight. Carvers who opted for lead fins or hanger brackets were killing two fish with one spear, as it were. Most makers, however, simply routed out cavities in the base of their decoys and added molten lead there. Given that the lanyard would be tied to the very top of the fish, it was better to have the weight as low in the decoy as possible anyway. "Floater" decoys, meant to stay at a certain depth, sometimes were anchored by drop weights, shaped like large casting sinkers, that sat on the lake bottom.

Although lots of old decoys are just straightforward, generic "fish," most were carved and/or painted to resemble specific food species. Curiously enough, many also mimic the kind of fish they were supposed to attract, and sometimes in sizes that might make even a giant muskie hesitate. Popular examples of the former include panfish–mostly humpbacked sunfish and crappies, or striped and streamlined perch–as well as dace, whitefish, chubs, smelts, shiners and carp. Suckers were a particular favorite too, along with the brook trout and lake trout that inhabited those cold northern waters. Less common were walleyes, various basses, catfish and bullheads, bowfins, lamprey eels and many, many others. In fact, the kinds of fish represented by decoys greatly outnumber the species that they were used to catch.

"Same-kind" decoys were mostly pike, pickerel, muskies or sturgeon, and a few were more than four feet long. The larger ones may have been a kind of confidence trick, a variant of the waterfowler's swan or snipe–hanging a wooden pike near a swimming bluegill decoy might trigger a rush from a real pike bent on reaching the morsel ahead of his competitor. Usually fish were used by themselves, however.

Decoys of predatory fish eating others–a pike with a perch in its mouth, for example–are becoming popular, but these are mostly contemporary decorative carvings.

Sturgeon decoys were popular in Wisconsin for sturgeon spearing, and they served an important secondary purpose. Sturgeon were rare fish even a generation and more ago, and protected by bag and length limits. To keep themselves on the right side of the law, carvers often made their sturgeon decoys exactly to the legal minimum length set for the real fish. When one swam into the picture, it was easy to compare it to the fake and act accordingly. There are a lot of 40-inch sturgeon decoys in Wisconsin to this day. The best ones are particularly fine folk art.

(To beat this analogy to death: Duck hunters often do something similar with their decoys–using a particular one to mark the edge of their effective shooting range. When a bird came inside that decoy, it was fair game.)

Predatory gamefish eat more than just fish, of course, and some old decoys were made to represent other animals. Among these, frogs were the most popular. Some were unrealistically large–frogs nearly a foot long were perhaps meant to be a pike's dream come true. There were plenty of other creatures too, including salamanders, crayfish, mice and turtles, and even, inexplicably, ducklings, dragonflies and butterflies (with working wings), the odd beaver or muskrat, and at least one bat. One of the rarest "fish" decoys, unearthed in Wisconsin recently, is a nearly life-size carved bufflehead duck. Buffleheads are divers, so this decoy (the body is hollow) is balanced and weighted to swim realistically under the ice. The bird has a single hanging loop on its lower back, and its webbed wooden feet are attached by snap swivels, to waggle freely. Large northern pike or muskies sometimes take ducks, so the idea isn't completely farfetched–even if the bird was badly out of season.

Labeling these as "fish decoys" isn't as misleading as it may sound. All spearing decoys are intended to lure fish within range, not merely imitate fish themselves. In general, few genuinely old "critter" decoys survive, and all of them are quite valuable.

OLD FISH decoys usually look old, but that in itself is no guarantee of authenticity. "Antique" dealers have long known how to age and distress reproductions to make them appear to be something they're not. Collectors have been known to hand a suspect decoy to a doctor friend for X-ray analysis down at the hospital. Contemporary decoy carvers—at least those who trouble to call themselves that—are, in the eyes of many true-blue collectors, "merely" artists who create display items, even if their decoys are used occasionally for spearing. Modern decoy makers also like variety. (One of the best, Bob Beebe, has even made a run of a hundred striped bass decoys. Legitimate, I suppose, since stripers have moved into fresh water very successfully.) Modern carvings can be masterful works, painted and shaped to the finest detail, stunningly lifelike and far too delicate, not to say expensive, for field chores. They belong on sideboards, mantels or under glass. They are sporting art—not folk art and certainly not fishing tackle.

Authentic spearing decoys are often not only old, they're also battered. Hours spent in freezing water took their toll on paint and wood alike. Aggressive, toothy fish sometimes left their mark too, as did badly aimed fish spears. And the makers themselves changed and repainted their decoys continually, like fly tiers looking for that super-killer pattern that no fish could resist. To collectors, these are all badges of honor.

Native Americans, Eskimo and Indian, made the first fish decoys, simple shapes in wood, shell, bone or antler, and they passed the method on to white settlers. However, the true heyday of the working fish decoy came in the early decades of this century—particularly the Depression, when men had time on their hands and mouths to feed. Those carvers were fishermen first, and few of them ever went into any sort of commercial production or adopted a formal trademark. The fisherman made his own decoys his own way, just as he built his own ice shanty, rigged his own lines, cleaned and ate his own catch. That's why it can be impossible to identify or even age a particular decoy—at least so far. Spiralling auction prices and increasing interest always spur research onward, and as old newspaper clippings and the notebooks, letters and other effects of carvers come to light, what we know about spearing decoys keeps expanding.

A few of the better carvers, those with an aptitude for it, or whose fish swam particularly well or looked particularly enticing, did sometimes make decoys to sell or to trade, just as some anglers tied flies for others.

COLLECTORS today largely agree that Oscar ("Pelee") Peterson was the master of the hand-carved decoy trade. He was born to Swedish parents in 1887, in Grayling, Michigan, and lived mostly in Cadillac until he died in 1951. His life's output has been estimated at 25,000 or more carvings, by no means all of which were spearing decoys. He also did an incredible variety of larger decorative fish, plaques and signs, as well as oddities ranging from wooden fish vases and canoe pincushions to animals and human figures. He sold, gave or bartered these widely to stores, restaurants, filling stations, sports shops, his decoy customers, even taverns—as payment for bar tabs, some say. Decoy experts divide his work into five distinct periods, distinguished by variations in shape or hardware, and rate it accordingly. Regardless of period, many of his fish share a certain similarity of shape: Whether they're shiners or pike, trout or suckers, they are generally slim and streamlined, and gracefully and gently curved in one direction (occasionally the tail curves back the other way), from the head back to the integral wooden tail. Holding one gives you the sensation of cradling a real life-form, one that's gone unresistingly to sleep for a moment. The lower jaw typically juts out ahead of the upper, and the tail forks very little, if at all. What really sets many Peterson decoys apart, however, is their paint. For whatever reason, Oscar seemed to favor bold, bright, almost (but not quite) garish colors–starting with the mouths of most of his fish, which he painted lipstick-red. From there back, he stuck more or less to representational coloring, giving perch their vertical stripes, trout their spots and so on. But what stylish stripes and spots! The brook trout, with the vermiculations on their backs and their spotted sides, are sheer delights to look at. Today some of Peterson's carvings rank among the finest and truest American folk art, and although the decoys currently bring $500 to $3,000 or more, some experts feel they are undervalued still. Many of them the maker probably sold for less than a dollar. For sheer, stunning impact, nothing beats Peterson's three-dimensional fish signs that hung in bait shops. Peterson authority Ron Fritz writes that presently four of these have been located, and the hunt is on for others that appear in old photographs. They are superbly painted and detailed, down to their individually carved teeth, and the collector who turns one up may well thank his stars.

The Janner family of Mount Clemens, Michigan made unique decoys also, and they too have become very valuable. Hans Janner, the patriarch, often made fins for his decoys from the metal tags on parts made by the General Fire Truck Company. Sometimes he cut them so that they read "Gener," thus phonetically signing his name. Hans's son, Augie, also a carver, worked for the highway department and brought home roadside reflectors for them to make fish eyes with. Hans had a son-in-law too, named Andy Trombley, who also earned a reputation for fine working decoys. He would stretch hair net over his fish and then spray-paint the mesh to produce a scale pattern.

FISH DECOYS, reasoned a few tackle manufacturers, are only oversize fishing lures, and consequently put "factory fish," as collectors sometimes call them, into production. James Heddon's Sons and the South Bend Bait Company both transformed some of their existing plugs into "ice decoys" by swapping the treble hooks for metal fins and tails–leaving, in a few cases, the swivel eye or propeller blade in place. Creek Chub, Paw Paw, Pflueger and perhaps Shakespeare also made spearing decoys, but apparently never in great quantities or varieties. In the Midwest, where the demand was greatest, a few companies sprang up that took the opposite tack–mass-producing decoys and turning out few, if any lures. "Mass" production is something of a relative term here. The Bear Creek Bait Company, which still offers its Ice King decoys, is a true factory, as was the Randall operation in Willmar, Minnesota; but at the other end of the scale were outfits like Cy's Fish Decoy Company (also of Willmar) and various tackle shops that produced small runs of their own fish. And a couple of hand-carvers went through mass-production phases also–in fact, given Oscar Peterson's astonishing output, it could be argued that he was a factory unto himself.

Some of these commercial fish were wood, but many were metal, rubber or, more recently, plastic. (Ice King fish started out in wood, then in the 1950s became plastic and over the years developed such modern touches as fluorescent finishes.) They may lack some of the appeal of the hand-carved, one-off fish, but keep an open mind. Unlike one-offs, they often came in cardboard boxes, which themselves can be decorative and valuable. Factory decoys from the major lure makers, those who figure prominently in antique plug collections, are scarce and highly collectible; fortunately, their histories are usually better known.

A DEALER'S display at an outdoor swap meet. The maker of the brook trout, rear, may have been influenced by the style of Oscar Peterson.

OSCAR PETERSON decoys. Bottom to top: A handsome nine-inch-long northern pike • A "Period II" shiner decoy, eight inches long, with tack eyes • Seven-inch sucker, identified as early Period III • Also a seven-inch sucker; this one, however, experts classify as Period IV.

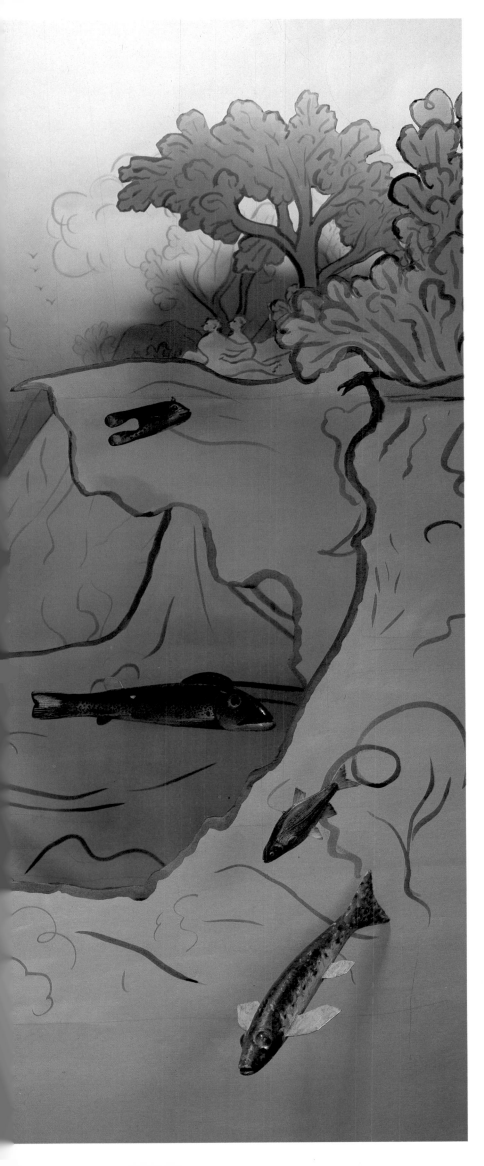

THESE CLASSIC *spearfishing decoys include a leather-tailed New York fish (center, rear) • A pair of Oscar Peterson decoys, at upper right, one of which is a rare frog • Three perch carved by Isaac Goulette, at upper left • And fish by both Hans and Augie Janner, with sign-reflector eyes. Photograph by Lisa Charles; with permission of Art & Antiques Magazine.*

EARLY AND late Oscar Peterson decoys, both highly characteristic. The perch is seven inches; the Period IV smelt, nine inches, is in particularly good condition.

A FINE twelve-inch shad decoy, carved by Hans Janner, Sr. The wood is walnut, his favorite, and the fins are copper. Janner Senior, who worked in the 1920s, produced very few decoys; all are valuable.

OF OSCAR Peterson's working decoys, many collectors regard the various brook trout as his finest. The smaller fish measures 5 3/4 inches; the other is nine inches. Both are Period IV, in excellent condition.

THIS 10 1/2-INCH brook trout from the late 1930s is one of the largest known of Jim Nelson's decoys. He lives in Cadillac, Michigan, and made decoys for some forty years. Nelson's paint jobs sometimes outshine even Peterson, who undoubtedly had an influence on him. Not only the mouth but also the gills and the underside of the body are carved.

UNKNOWN MAKERS. *The primitive perch at top has tack eyes and a dorsal fin of wire screen; the other fins are copper • By contrast, the bluegill, with its striped tail, looks almost whimsical. It was probably made late in the 1940s.*

ISAAC GOULETTE, of New Baltimore, Michigan, made these wooden decoys probably in the 1930s. The perch at top, with a carved tail and metal fins, measures about 5 3/4 inches. The other two are suckers. Isaac's father, Abe Goulette, also carved spearing decoys.

DECOYS FROM unknown carvers. At top is a leather-tail fish from Lake Chatauqua, New York, 6 3/4 inches long, with carved mouth and gills • The center fish has bead eyes plus metal fins and a carved tail • The bottom fish has both tail and fins made of tin.

NINE-INCH long fish by Louie Leach, of Fairmont, Minnesota, who died in 1982. His carved wooden "glitter" decoys had a great reputation as fish-getters, and were widely sought. Most were reputedly white and black with red heads, and most have the initials "LL" in the belly. The eyes are flathead copper tacks, and the tails are reinforced with sheet-metal tabs that wrap around the body.

THESE TWO early decoys were carved in moose antler by Chippewa Indians of the Rama Reserve, in Rama, Ontario.

METAL DECOYS, *including an unusual riveted crappie with copper eyes. One side is stamped "Wolf Lake Decoy"; the other side reads "M. Kuha."* • *The silver-color fish with the red "jewel" eyes is another rarity—hand-cast aluminum, and apparently (to judge by its weight) solid. It was made in Minnesota* • *The copper fish is hollow, with holes to let water in so the decoy will sink; 10 1/2 inches overall, it is a typical find (and valuable) Charlie Slecta "copper." Slecta lived in Wayzata, Minnesota, and he learned the sheet-metal trade in the body shop at the Ford Motor Company.*

THIS PLAIN but well made and proportioned muskie is 15 1/2 inches long; the eyes are brass tacks, and the fins and tail are copper. It came from Minnesota, but the carver is unknown. The four small shiner decoys were made in Bay City, Michigan, in the 1920s, by D.C. Revit.

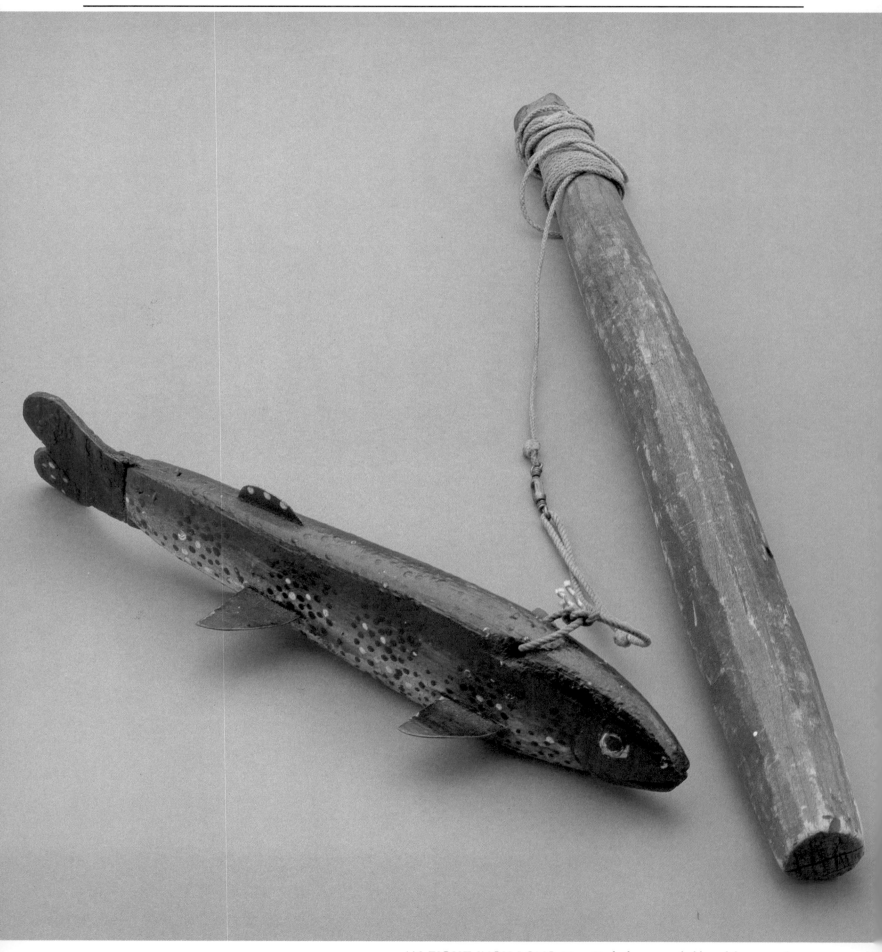

AN EIGHT-INCH-LONG *New York decoy, probably a lake trout, believed to date from very early in this century. It has a characteristic leather tail and the jigging stick and twine appear original. The maker is unknown.*

ART &
ACCESSORIES

MY OWN FAVORITE fishing "collectible" is not a fine cane rod or a turn-of-the-century bass reel. Nor is it a Peterson brook trout or a Haskell Minnow. It is a gaff. A hand gaff. It's about two feet long, with a smallish hand-forged steel hook. The haft, however, is bamboo–hexagonal split Tonkin cane, of a diameter and strength that was used in medium-heavy salmon/salt–water fly rods a generation ago. Both the handle and the ferrule that joins the bamboo to the hook are solid sections of high-grade aluminum alloy. These were lovingly, and lavishly, shaped and knurled on a lathe before being fitted, glued and pinned to the cane and the hook. The butt cap of the handle is drilled for a lanyard, which was braided from flag halyard and attached with a decorative knot. The final touch was a carved cork-and-wood guard to protect the sharp point. The whole thing makes about as much sense as a solid-gold cuspidor–too much care bestowed upon an item of plain-jane utility. In fact, the last time I saw the gaff, the hook was rusty, the guard was missing, and the cane badly needed buffing. I think I know where it is now, and I hope to get it back.

Strictly speaking, the gaff is not a collectible. It has little or no value to anyone else. It doesn't have a desirable telescoping brass handle, nor is it threaded to mount on a rod case or net handle as part of a fancy angling set. It didn't belong to anyone famous, or assist in any record-book catches. The workmanship is good but not outstanding, and the maker was no one famous. In fact, I made it myself. Today I'd like to have it on a bookshelf in my study, to remind myself of the way things were in a time gone by.

Is that not what collectibles should do for us? Haven't you ever held an old and worn–but obviously cared for–gun, knife or sword, and silently willed it to talk? To spill its guts, tell you its story, the deeds it shared in, by whose side it rode into battle and what lives it saved (or took)? Fishing gear may have no less a story to tell, and the most mundane articles can become significant and collectible: On a mantel in Florida I saw a battered box of Cuban cigars that reputedly sailed with Ernest Hemingway out of Havana, on the *Pilar*, his fishing boat.

Pictured in this chapter is a handsome leather-covered case fitted full of intricate compartments and boxes containing the "fishing effects" of one L.P. Thompson, who lived (according to the engraved plaque in the lid) in Newton Centre, Massachusetts. It contains a diary entitled "Trout Stream Insects," and it begins with number 35, suggesting that Mr. Thompson had been fishing since well before the inscribed date, which is 1920. The tackle itself suggests the same—it is well used and was well maintained, and it is of a quality and selection that further suggests Thompson knew what he was about and appreciated the best. There are salmon and trout patterns, including a number of excellent dry flies, and two fine reels. One of the small fly boxes reads on its lid, "Floating Hackles, Series of 1919, Designed by L.P. Thompson, Tied by Hardy Bros." It was not unusual for companies such as Hardy's to custom-make special flies for its clients—they and many others still do, in fact—but it is less usual for the client to design the patterns himself. Thompson did know what he was doing.

To another fisherman, looking through this assortment is not unlike paging through Thompson's family photo album. There are a hundred clues to his style, intelligence, wordly status and angling skills. No single item in there is particularly valuable. To the sensitive collector, however, the entire collection is worth a good deal more than the sum of all its parts. They represent a life in its context, like a fish in its aquatic environment. Sifting through those things, mulling over their significance, can be a task Sherlock Holmes himself might find pleasurable.

BEYOND personal significance, there is angling history. Collectors often regard themselves as the curators of the development of their particular game, and this is no less true in fishing than in French Impressionist art. Take, for instance, fishing lines. They are as central to the whole idea of fishing as any item that earned its own chapter in this book—such as rods and reels—and a good deal more important than decoys or lures. Some say we can trace every major, overall improvement in fishing (there haven't been many), those giant-steps in both tackle and technique, to breakthroughs in line technology. Vegetable fibers such as flax, or horse hair, strands of silk, gut (literally, intestine; usually from dead silkworms, which can produce strong, fine strands up to twenty inches long), various metal wires, and then all the synthetics, singly and in combination: Perlon, nylon, Dacron, polyester, vinyl with microballoons, Kevlar and so on and on. The diameter, tensile strength, suppleness and longevity of our fishing line affects almost every other choice we make: the size and strength of the rod, the type, capacity and drag system of the reel, the size of the lure and its hook and how it's to be presented, and so on. The only decision more basic is what kind of fish to go after, which itself determines the line we'll use. And, as it happened, for centuries many fish were effectively uncatchable because there were no lines strong enough, yet fine enough, to take them on.

A strand of horsehair reportedly has a tensile strength of about two pounds, while best-quality silkworm gut might exceed 15 pound test. The cotton "threadline" used on Illingworth's spinning reel was in the single-horsehair category. Theoretically, very strong lines could be produced just be weaving together more and more strands. In fact, however, diameters soon became awkwardly bulky, making the line stiff, reducing reel capacity, and even frightening the fish. This last problem could be reduced by using a fine, tapered leader (a "cast," to the British) between the lure and a heavy line, but the point of diminishing returns appeared quickly here as well. Because of its relatively high strength-per-thickness, gut was favored for leaders, but the leader is always the weak link in any heavy-duty line "chain." There's no point in using a 50 pound line if it could only be fished with a 15 pound leader tippet. Until synthetic fibers came along, then, casting lines–of braided silk, for suppleness–were limited to about 35 pound test, and that already had a diameter of forty thousandths of an inch. Salt–water lines, used to troll (not cast) for huge gamefish, could be much thicker; the best non-synthetics were braided or twisted linen, and rated according to the number of threads. A wet six thread linen line was 18 pound test; a 72 thread line was 216 pound test.

It takes a particularly keen collector to go after antique lines. There are some, of course. Collectors, that is. Few truly antique lines have survived–pre-dating silk, let's say–because they were so susceptible to rotting or, in the opposite case, drying up and cracking or crumbling away. Naturally, even before that could happen, insects or mice might chew them up.

Interestingly, though, an avid collector, or fisherman with an inquiring mind, can make and use his own "antique" fishing lines. There's likely no better way to appreciate how much fishing meant to our ancestors than by putting ourselves through that process. Silk fly lines, braided and tapered, are still used today and still commercially available, as they have been since before the turn of the century, but they're hardly common. Each new one, in a way, is already a collectible. And linen lines were still being made until about 1960. But to create your own antique line, the directions are still available in 19th century angling books and periodicals, and modern magazines occasionally reprint them for everyone's amazement. And it's still not too difficult to come up with a bundle of hair. Most of those old texts recommend light-colored strands from the tail of a stallion. They have to be picked, sorted for length and quality, washed, dried and then braided together into "links," which in turn were knotted end-to-end to make up the entire fishing line.

The machine that was invented to twist the strands evenly together is as close as most tackle collectors ever get to antique lines, and in truth they're much more interesting to look at and display than a length of line. Such mechanical line-winders were used for perhaps two centuries, so it's no surprise that they're still routinely uncovered at flea markets and tackle auctions, and for very reasonable prices. The device is a disc-shaped box, often brass, with three hooks or pins protruding from one side and a crank handle on the other. There was a large clamp or screw attached to the thing as well, for mounting it on a table or even a tree stump. Strands of hair were attached to each hook and tied together and weighted at the other end. The fisherman then slowly worked the crank, which turned the hooks through internal gears and twisted the fibers together, while he guided their progress with a grooved block of cork or wood. Then he tied the ends off and stored that link in a pail of water while he laboriously twisted the next one, and so on until he had enough to knot together into a line. The truly compleat angler would then dye this line to the color of the water it would be fished in– in fact, he might already have selected his horsehair to some ratio like two white strands to one brown, to come closer to the finished color he wanted.

When commercial silk and linen lines finally took over, in the early years of this century, line winding machines were replaced by even more bizarre-looking line driers. An organic line had to be unspooled from the reel and dried after use, or it would rot. Driers had four or six arms arranged like spokes of a rimless wheel, a foot or less across, which could be turned with a crank handle. The angler simply wound the line off his reel onto the arms of the drier, and left it there until it was time to go fishing again. Then he just wound it back onto the reel. Large driers could be clamped to a table, or came already fixed to a board, to which the reel could also be mounted in series. Sometimes they were ornate affairs, made of furniture-grade wood and decked out with brass fittings, and some had adjustable-length arms, to take up more or less line. At the other extreme, many tackle companies offered small hand-held folding driers, with reel seats right on their handles.

Until rot-proof nylon and Dacron came along, every serious fisherman had a line drier of one sort or another, and new ones are still available for fly fishermen who choose to stick with silk lines. Antique driers are intriguing reminders of the "old days," good or otherwise, and they are still widely available at prices within the reach of every collector.

FISH PRIESTS, modern ones anyway, are becoming harder to find in America as catch-and-release fishing gains momentum. Among those who still keep fish as a matter of course, fresh–water meat hunters aren't usually concerned with killing their catch cleanly, and that leaves salt–water fishermen and tradition-minded salmon anglers. Certain marine fish are just too big or too toothy to hang on a stringer or leave flapping in the bottom of a boat, so "priests"–billy clubs–are common on charter boats to administer the "last rites." In Europe still, Atlantic salmon are invariably killed for the table. These great fish contain much blood, and to improve the flavor of their meat salmon are often stuck and bled like slaughtered pigs. Cleanly despatching the noble trophy first is almost a ritual, and while a river rock applied to the top rear of the head does the job nicely, salmon anglers who live the sport carry their own priests.

Trout fishermen everywhere regard themselves as a higher form of sportsman, unwilling to let their quarry gasp and flop about in pain, and wherever trout were (or still are) killed, priests–if only a suitable length of a branch–were common.

Antique, purpose-made priests can be surprisingly handsome and interesting collectibles. Clearly, a lot of thought and design went into the balance and shape of some of them, and even the six-inch pocket-size versions can be quite deadly. Many were brass or stainless steel, and had wrist lanyards and knurled or turned grips for a secure hold. Fancy ones were sometimes made for important personages, in ivory or ebony, occasionally even engraved or chased with silver. Wooden priests usually have molten lead (or perhaps shot) poured into a cavity in the head.

The fisherman's mythical inventiveness was applied to clubs too–some had a hook disgorger built into the handle, and undoubtedly somewhere there's a priest with a gutting knife concealed inside. A few pocket gaffs had knobbed or weighted handles that doubled as priests. Farlow's of London offered a "Meakin" priest that was supposed to free lures stuck on the bottom. Made of unweighted wood, it had a split ring on the handle, into which the snagged line could be slipped; then the fisherman let the club slide along the line to the water, where it was supposed to float downstream of the hang-up and free the hook by tugging from the opposite direction. It may even have worked occasionally.

"Tackle releasers," it should be noted, were fashionable in the 1920s and '30s. Some, like the Meakin priest, were the floating type; Hardy's sold one, called the Silver Devon, that was somewhat boat-shaped, presumably to swim downstream better. Others were concave wooden discs weighted with lead keels; they rode upright in the water, and their dished sides were meant to provide more pull against the current. There were sinking lure retrievers too, resembling heavy clasp bracelets, that slid down the line and engaged the snagged hooks. Then they were pulled to the surface with the heavy line attached.

Finally, to recover lures and flies snagged in an overhanging tree branch, fishermen could buy a "clearing knife." This was a heavy-duty flat steel hook, sharpened like a knife on the inside of its notch, and with a hole and a small pin or peg. The hole was for a length of line; the peg fit into the tiptop guide on a fishing rod. To use it, the fisherman hoisted it up on his rod and hooked the notch over the offending branch. Then—in principle—a sharp tug on the line would cut the branch and free the lure (or at least bring the branch down within reach). Fancier versions could be mounted onto a special net handle and used for clearing brush. The idea has been around for perhaps a century, and it seems to get revived once every generation or so. At least one version has just been reintroduced to the market in 1989.

THE FISHERMAN'S KNIFE can be a highly sought-after item, but it generally gets this respect and attention only from knife collectors. The reason may be that a good knife is such an all-purpose thing that distinguishing one meant specifically for fishing can be difficult. Tackle buffs seem more likely to lump knives into the general category of fishing tools—the various combination gadgets beloved of anglers everywhere.

Knives that were specifically made for fresh-water sportfishing are almost always folders, which have been around since the 18th century, and essentially variants on the "modern" Swiss Army knife—which itself dates back to about 1890. Most carry at least one basic blade, with a point shaped for gutting, and a screwdriver. To be a fishing knife, there should also be some sort of hook disgorger (that may double as a file and/or a fish scaler), often a pair of folding scissors and, for picking knots apart, a stout needle. Fancier versions might also offer a corkscrew, for those inclined to leisurely streamside lunches. Larger folding knives, intended to be carried in a pocket or belt sheath, could be decked out with mother-of-pearl handle scales, while the more compact and lightweight versions—fitted with lanyard loops, to hang from a vest or tackle bag—had flat steel sides, often with inches or hook sizes marked on them.

Most of the commercial knife makers of America at one time or another made some form of fishing knife, and many are relatively recent. Super-specialization in knife design is a contemporary phenomenon that didn't really shift into high gear until after World War I, when a pioneering knifesmith named William Scagel began turning out specially shaped blades for all sorts of specific uses.

Today, fishing knives are a dime a dozen, and almost every major tackle and knife company has jumped on the bandwagon, usually with some sort of fillet knife aimed at the salt-water meat fisherman. More appropriately called fish knives, they're distinguished mostly by the length of their blades and their various non-slip synthetic handle materials. Several models have interchangeable blades, but overall very few are interesting enough, or made well enough, ever to qualify as collectible. Handcrafted knives, though, are another story entirely. There are hundreds of smiths at work in the United States now, making limited numbers of knives that range from good to fabulous in materials, design and craftsmanship, and naturally some of them have turned their abilities toward fishing knives. Unlike the mass-produced antiques, these are normally fixed-blade sheath knives, and they are "fishing" types because of some design element—a lanyard loop/gut scoop, for example, or a sharp notch ground into the choil, for cutting monofilament.

One of the most unusual and best-made fishing knives of all, however, is a heavy all-steel folder that is still being produced, by Puma of West Germany. Called the Scale Knife, it has a single large blade that's notched along its upper edge, but these notches aren't for removing fish scales. Instead, this is a *weight* scale. The knife is intended to hang from the leather thong on its bail; then a fish is hung, by a loop of line, from one of the notches in the blade. Move the fish back and forth along the blade until the whole knife hangs level, and then read the fish's weight off a scale on the blade. Along with being a reasonably accurate balance beam, it also happens to be a very high-quality knife, capable of holding a shaving-sharp edge, and the big counterweight knob on the end of the handle makes an effective priest.

Fishing scales often figure in general tackle collections. Antique versions, usually British or European, are typically hollow brass cylinders with a handle loop on one end and a hook at the other; a piston inside compresses a coil spring when a load is hung on the hook, and a peg slides along a graduated scale to indicate the weight.

LANDING NETS have changed little over the centuries they've been in use. There have been some variations in materials and in design, but the basics remain basic. Handles, long, short and telescoping, have been made of every imaginable material, from bamboo (whole culms as well as split-and-glued) to aluminum, while the bow might be anything from flexible whalebone (baleen, that is) to split ash. Bows haven't always been completely round or oval, either; nets with Y-shaped handle ferrules have been with us since at least the 1880s.

The big drawback to a landing net is its awkward size, and clever fishermen have been inventing ways around this for generations. Nets with collapsible hoops (triangular net heads are particularly easy to fold down), folding or detachable handle ferrules, and takedown or telescopic handles have been around for more than a century. Convenience wasn't always a consideration, however. In regions where gentleman anglers fished with paid guides or ghillies—usually meaning trout or salmon rivers—nets could reach gargantuan dimensions. Still today, in Norway or Maritime Canada, guides often use steel-bowed nets with handles six feet long and four or five inches square, and with bags that may be four feet deep and a yard across at the mouth. One of these huge contemporary nets, in suitably used condition, makes an excellent backdrop for a collection of older fishing tackle—if, that is, you can get it home in one piece.

Some of the most esthetically pleasing small hand nets are being made today, by craftsmen like Chris Brodin, who laminate and steam-bend several kinds of wood together to form oval shapes as subtle and graceful as violins. The most interesting landing nets, however, are probably those 19th century versions that were part of a complete angling kit. The net bow could be screwed into a ferrule on the end of a rod-tip case, which then became the net handle. (Gaff heads were also set up this way.)

Old net bags don't always hold up as well as the frames, since they were normally knotted from cotton cord or even braided silk. Depending on the quality of the craftsmanship and materials, any net may be collectible, in the sense of worth owning; no net, however, will ever command the sort of prices that prize reels, rods and lures do.

WADERS would seem to be modern inventions, yet in fact they date back 150 years or more and for that reason alone probably deserve more attention from collectors than they get. Waterproof boots, no matter how high, aren't overwhelmingly interesting, however; there are no moving parts, no evidence of brilliant design or mechanical engineering or impressive craftsmanship. Yet rubber waders, like aluminum reels and nylon fishing line, heralded significant technological advances that affected almost every aspect of our culture.

Rubber—natural rubber, distilled from latex, the sap of the rubber tree—had been known in Europe since at least 1530, when an Italian explorer, just back from the New World, South America, published his journals. In 1736, a Frenchman named Charles Marie de la Condamine described to his disbelieveing peers back home the one-piece waterproof rubber boots that he'd seen Amazon Indians making and wearing. Shortly afterward latex was brought to Europe and development began. By 1791, a few perceptive anglers may have gotten a hint of things to come, for in that year a Mr. Samuel Peel obtained a patent for using liquid rubber to waterproof materials such as leather, cotton and linen. The commercial rubber industry was born.

In 1820 the Thomas Hancock Company was founded in London, and became the first large-scale manufacturer of rubber products. Three years later Charles Macintosh invented a superior means of coating fabrics with rubber and himself went into the business. Although he later merged with Hancock, the term "Mackintosh," with a K added, came to mean any waterproof form of clothing.

Over the next 20 years, most of the new rubber companies died almost as quickly as they were formed. Rubber had a very serious drawback—in winter it went stiff and in summer it became sticky. Eventually an American, Charles Goodyear, accidentally solved the problem with a curing process that stabilized rubber in normal temperatures. Overseas, the Hancock Company was awarded the British patent in 1843, and Goodyear got around to patenting his process, called vulcanization, in the States a year later. Now the way was clear, and sportsmen everywhere were soon revelling in relatively lightweight waterproof hats, coats, leggings and boots.

Continental fishermen apparently began taking wading equipment for granted almost as soon as it became available. One of the first mentions of such gear in print is this casual aside from Thomas Stoddardt's *The Angler's Companion to the Rivers and Lochs of Scotland:* "It would be quite superfluous were I to enumerate the different descriptions of India-Rubber wading boots, which, from time to time, have been submitted to my inspection." (It seems leaks were a problem even then, for Stoddardt goes on to say that, although staying dry while fishing is a boon in his advancing years, he prefers leather waterproofs to rubber, as the former are sturdier. Here he is almost certainly referring to knee-high rather than chest-high boots.)

The angling literature of the next 30 years doesn't tell us when chest waders were actually invented, but in an 1882 issue of *The American Angler* recommends, in part:
"For wading a brook in early spring, Scotch MacKintosh wading pants should be used, fitting over the feet like stockings. The body should be large enough for the coat skirts to go inside, and should come nearly up to the armpits; over the feet outside the waterproofs should be worn a pair of heavy knit woolen socks to prevent the shoes from chafing a hole in the rubber. Later in the season the wading

pants should be discarded, as too warm and worse than useless."

If this sounds startlingly current, well, it was part of a column entitled, "Modern Fishing Tackle and How to Use It." The author went on to advise that no belt be worn over the "wading pants," so that perspiration may escape, and that the reader carry a wading staff (made of hollow bamboo, that also serves as a rod case). Alter a few words of terminology, and the same column could have (and probably did) run every spring in every fishing magazine for the next century.

Chest-high waders became popular in the 1880s. Goodyear's India Rubber Glove Manufacturing Company took a half-page ad in the 1886 *Sportsmen's Journal* that shows rubber "wading stockings and trousers." In its catalog of 1888, the H.H. Kiffe Co., of Brooklyn, makes it clear that fishing "stockings" were what we could call stockingfoot hip boots, and fishing pants were stockingfoot chest waders. The material they were made of was simply called "MacKintosh"–a rubber-coated fabric of some sort. The user wore hobnailed brogues with them.

Chest waders reached their final development, at least in appearance, in America in the 1920s, thanks to a young M.I.T. graduate named Mitchell Kaufman. He bought the already venerable Hodgman Rubber Company and moved it from Tuckahoe, New York, to Framingham, Massachusetts. There, in the search for lighter, stronger, more leakproof and durable outdoor footwear, Hodgman engineers produced the first integral-boot chest waders. Just like some of the bootfoot waders available today from Hodgman and other companies, these had a relatively lightweight fabric-base upper attached to a separately manufactured rubber boot, assembled in layers by hand on a shoemaker's last and then vulcanized in a curing oven. The resultant line of Red Ball rubber boots and waders earned a worldwide reputation for comfort and durability that endures to the present, despite the fact that production moved to the Far East some time in the 1970s.

I have never seen waders that pre-date the 1940s. All natural-rubber products eventually break down, become brittle and crack, when exposed to ozone, and this certainly took its toll. Waders also tend to get torn and patched, used up and then discarded; the idea of allowing old waders to retire honorably to a spot on the mantel or the wall–like a reel or a fine rod–seems ludicrous. On the other hand . . . .

In *The Fishing Gazette* of May 30, 1896, appeared an illustration of something called the Layman Pneumatic Boat, a classic piece of Victorian invention that would be recognized instantly by fishermen (and hunters) of today as a bellyboat, or float tube. It consisted of a pair of bootfoot chest waders, complete with front pocket and suspenders, with a large inflatable rubber doughnut attached at the waist. Like modern float tubes it boasted grab handles, a secondary air chamber at the back for extra flotation where it was needed, both foot and hand pumps, folding foot-fins for propulsion in the water, and a compact backpack carrying case. It was meant for fishing and also for waterfowling–the doughnut had sockets spaced around its circumference into which the hunter stuck poles that supported a blind of rushes and reeds. It differs from today's bellyboats only in that the tube and waders are apparently one piece. A drawing of a hunter wearing it in the woods shows the tube itself deflated and belted compactly around his waist.

Now *there's* a collector's item. I can see it in my mind, inflated and standing like a suit of armor in the corner of my study, supported by some sort of framework–or perhaps with a life-size figure inside, the figure completely decked out in the angling regalia of 1900.

FLY-TYING VISES are relatively recent innovations, dating from the closing years of the 1800s; before that hooks were simply held in the fingers, or perhaps jabbed into a stump or wooden tabletop, while the materials and thread were wound on. Until well into this century, many professional tiers regarded a mechanical vise as an amateur's crutch.

(In his 80s, Lee Wulff can still tie even tiny trout flies in his fingers, and he demonstrates at every session of his fly-fishing school in New York's Beaverkill Valley. One of those flies, it hardly needs saying, is an item of value all by itself.)

Early fly-tying vises were almost always screw-operated; that is, a thumbscrew opened and closed the jaws, just like a mechanic's or woodworker's full-size vise. Many had clamps to mount the vise on a fly-tying bench, but many tackle houses also offered compact hand vises that were meant to go into the field as part of the angler's kit. Some of these are quite interesting and attractive, particularly those made pre-plastic, before the drive to produce the most items at the least possible cost struck our society. Some were simple miniature clamps mounted on straight turned brass or wooden handles, but others were fitted with more intricate finger loops and rests to make them (supposedly, anyway) easier to hold without tiring or cramping.

These small vises were sometimes part of a fairly complete fly dresser's streamside outfit that might have been neatly packaged in a handcrafted, embossed-leather case. Tools accompanying the vise would have been one or more "fly-maker's tweezers," what we would call hackle pliers, and a dainty pair of surgical-quality scissors, often with a sheath or cap for the points. The compleat angler would likely round out this assortment with a bodkin, or stiletto needle, for unjamming knots or clearing hook eyes; a small sharpening file for hooks; tweezers that could serve as a hook disgorger; and probably a pair of small pliers, for snipping leader wire. In the early 1900s, various American and British firms also offered more general pocket-tool kits–assorted screwdrivers, sawblades, and files that stowed into a hollow carry case-handle that might be polished and knurled brass.

The fly-tying vise became "serious" tackle only very recently, when New Hampshire salmon-fly tier and tackle-shop owner Bill Hunter designed the HMH. In the late 1970s it became the first vise to break the hundred-dollar price barrier, and its cost drew howls of protest and snorts of derision from the competition. Fishermen, however, weren't listening, and bought the vises in steady numbers. The original HMH Premium, built and assembled under Hunter's direct supervision (he soon licensed the right to manufacture the HMH to another company), has become the most sought after vise of all. Reputedly only 341 of these were shipped, and their value is now five times or more the retail price. From the tier's standpoint, the current production lookalike HMH Standard is its equal as a tool (in fact, because of subtle improvements, the new ones are superior), but the "limited edition" syndrome applies to tying vises no less than it does to Bugatti Royales.

Two other modern vises–both are in regular, if very limited, production–that collectors should consider are the remarkable Renzetti Presentation and Ari T. Hart's unique travel vises. Andy Renzetti's hand-machined vise looks at first to be upside-down–the head seems to point the wrong way–but the logic of its design quickly becomes clear, and its workmanship, function, and materials are flawless. Its rotary head spins on needle bearings! ATH vises, made in Holland and Switzerland, fold compactly together and stow away in wooden cases. Seemingly everything on an ATH is adjustable and functional, and many of the vises even include a magnifying lens on its own standrod. Clever design, superb machining, and their look of industrial sculpture make these vises as noteworthy as the Renzettis, and any serious collector of fly-tying tools should acquire one of each while they're still available.

There are many collectible vises, however, that don't cost hundreds of dollars, and that are old–old for vises, that is. The period between the world wars produced many of these, simple tools from Noll, Herter's, Thompson and other companies. The most desirable are those that are mounted on boards with accessories such as thread holders and hackle clamps. One of the most unusual of the older vises is the Xuron, with its machined-steel head perched on a zig-zag standrod; the effect is that of a heron or stork. The design originated reportedly in France in the 1930s, and it was sold in the U.S.A. after World War II as the "Angler's Roost" or "Thomas" vise. In 1977, a New York tackle shop called the Bedford Sportsman offered a redesigned version, but the rights were sold soon after. It may again be produced by the new owners.

THE FIELD of antique angling miscellania could support a book unto itself, and fishermen's containers, in their tremendous variety and occasionally ingenious designs, could fill up several chapters. The creel, or fish basket, came–like so many other articles of fishing gear–to America from Britain. Once on these shores, however, the idea meshed perfectly with native traditions of basket weaving, and wicker type creels reached their ultimate state here in the early years of the 20th century. Leather creel and fish bags were more popular in Europe, but a few appeared in America as well; they must have been hell's own headache to carry when wet and loaded with fish, but they are eyecatching collectibles. Canvas creels, usually less attractive but equally valid as angling artifacts, came in many sizes; some even folded out to accommodate large fish. Old fly boxes and leader wallets, tackle boxes, lure holders, bait boxes, minnow traps and buckets and live wells have been made of almost every imaginable material–aluminum, leather, canvas, brass, wood, copper, glass–and in a range of sizes and shapes that may bewilder the collector. Even fishing vests, coats and shoulder bags all speak loudly of their own era and the fishing style of their users. The examples that crowd flea markets and auctions are often still full, too–flies, reels, spools, tools and other small items.

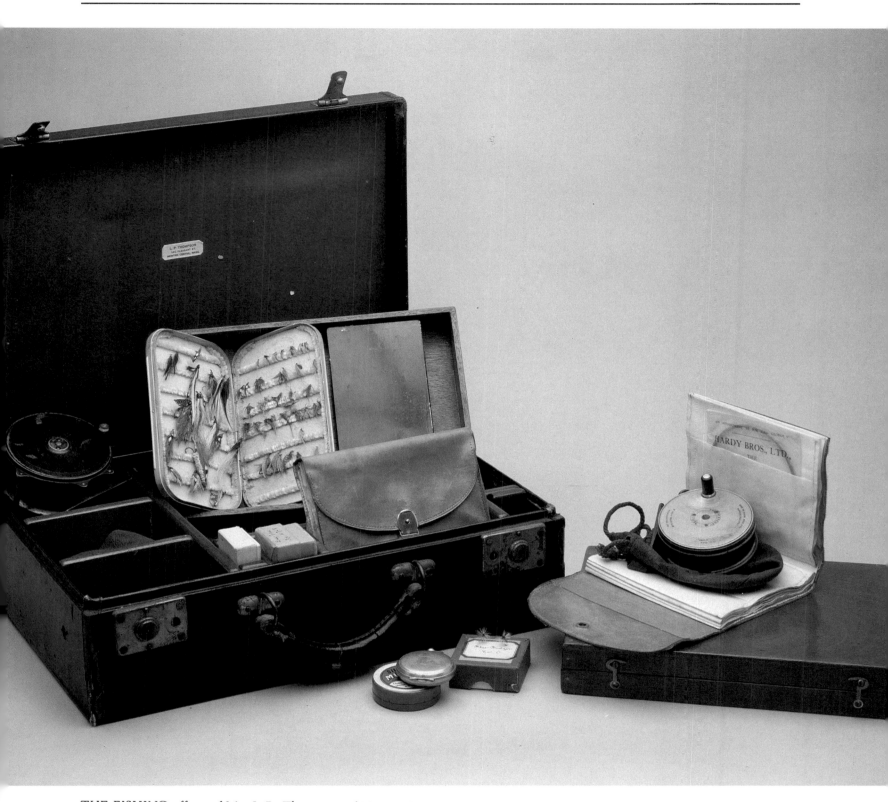

THE FISHING effects of Mr. L.P. Thompson, of Newton Centre, Massachusetts (according to the engraved plate in the lid). The 16x11x5-inch leather-covered carrying case holds an astonishing and varied collection of gear, including the Hardy Perfect fly reel (right), a brass raised-pillar salmon reel, a large lift-out wooden fly box and tray, two leather leader and tippet wallets, tins of line or fly dressings, and more than a dozen wood or cardboard boxes containing flies, hooks, tools, hackles and so on. The centerpiece, however, is Thompson's fishing diary, apparently not the first volume, which opens in 1920.

THIS TREMENDOUS, almost overstuffed, old leather fly book contains hundreds of excellent trout flies. An antique dealer might break it up in order to mount and frame select flies, or whole pages; the tackle collector would keep it intact; and the fisherman might just take it out on the stream.

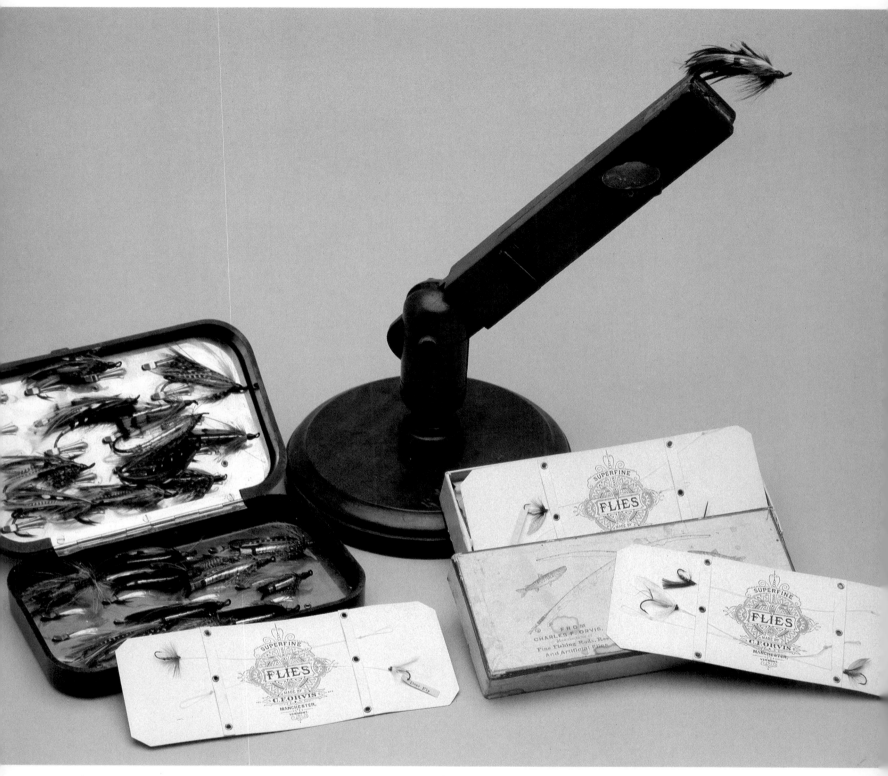

THE CENTERPIECE of this assortment is a rare 19th-Century wooden fly-tying vise with brass hinges and cork-faced jaws; the base has been hollowed out underneath and is weighted with lead. The fly box (6x3 3/4 inches) is a Hardy "Neroda," fitted with 40 clips and holding about two dozen classic salmon flies. The "Superfine" trout flies, on gut tippets, are early C.F. Orvis merchandise—eight cards in the original cardboard box.

COLLECTORS NOTE: The modern Renzetti Presentation vise is a limited-production item that is as functional and well-made as it is aesthetically pleasing. Photograph by Benjamin Magro.

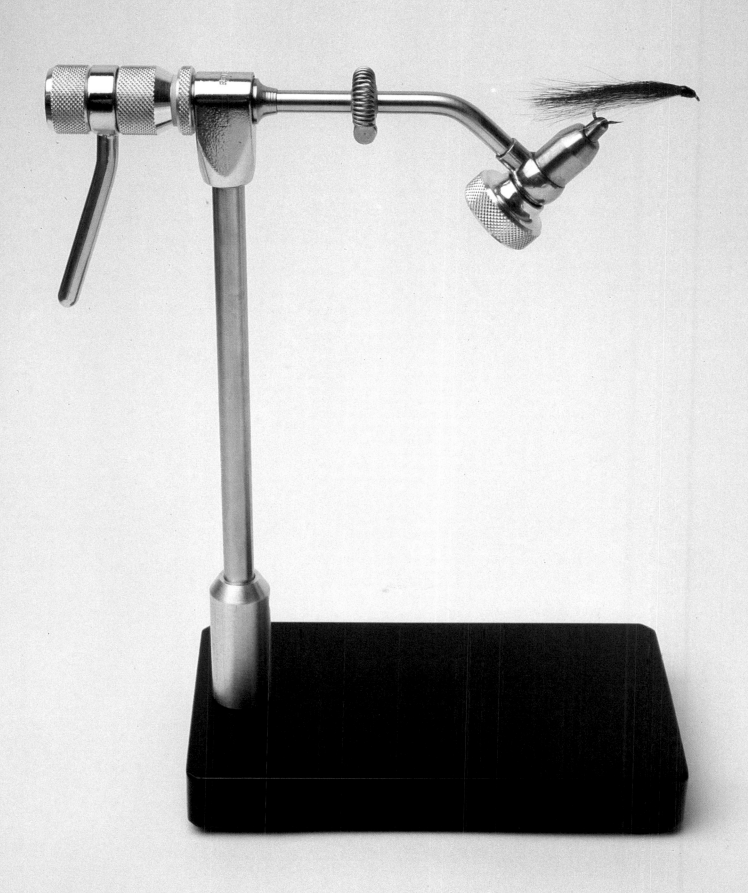

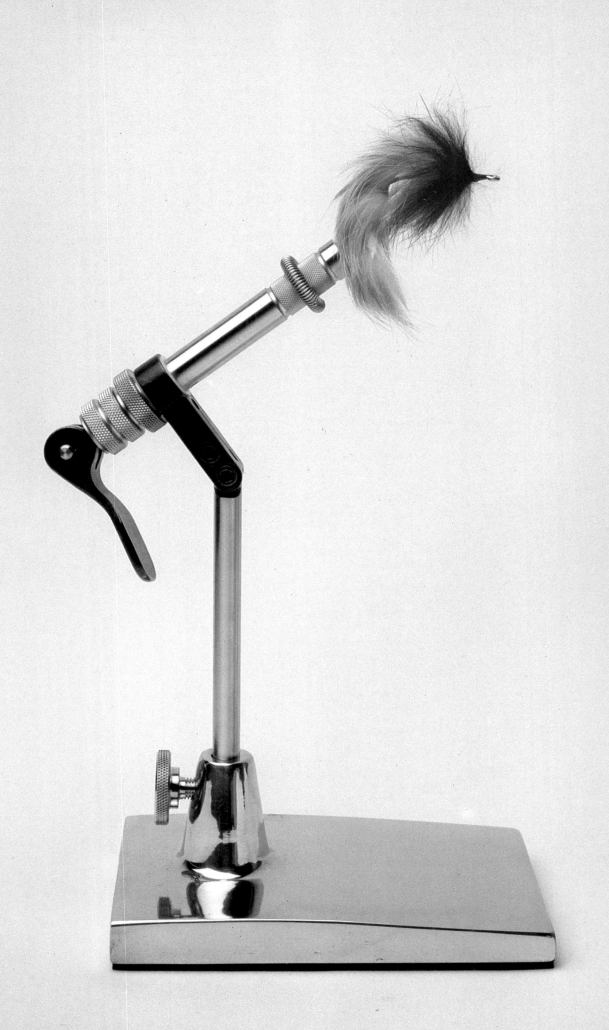

FOR THE *tackle collection that has everything: rare and unusual antique swim fins, of mahogany with leather and brass lacings and rings. Stamped "Dunlop," they were probably used to propel an early bellyboat.*

A MODERN *classic: The HMH Standard draw-cam fly-tying vise. Photograph by Benjamin Magro.*

THIS IS the sort of find that can reduce both collectors and salmon anglers to tears: an old, probably British, enameled-metal drop-front fly chest. This one measures 12 1/2x8 1/2x7 inches, and is fitted with twelve cork-lined drawers. When "discovered," it held about 125 full-dress salmon flies.

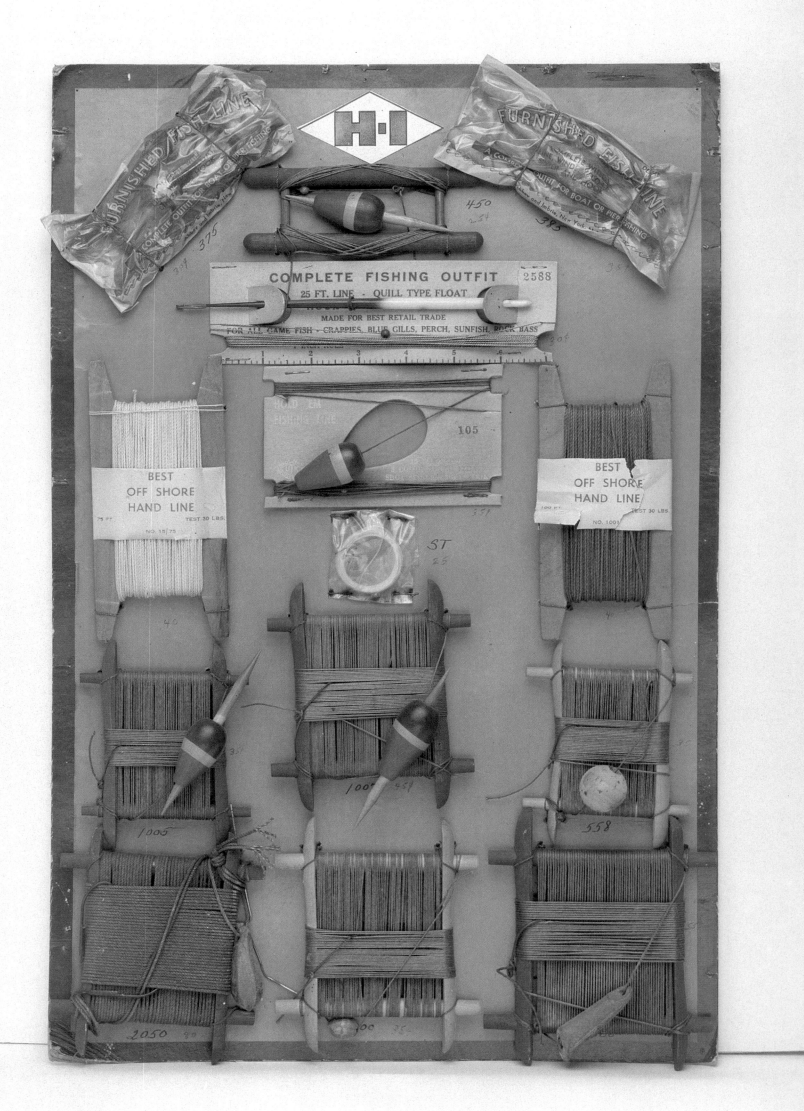

A BEAUTIFULLY *detailed and early brook trout by an unknown carver from Maine. The body of the fish is a laminate of three pieces of wood; the mount appears to be an old bread board.*

SHOP DISPLAYS, *such as this old dealer's board of 14 different H-I handlines, sinkers, and bobbers, can be colorful additions to any collection.*

ANOTHER FIRST-CLASS *find for the collector. This 12x9x5-inch stainless-steel fly chest has nine lift-out aluminum trays with 540 clips for large salmon flies— and some 250 flies. The handle plate is engraved "E.M. VOORHEES."*

THIS WONDERFUL old sewn birchbark creel (the white side of the bark faces inward) has leather hinges and a wooden toggle latch. Inside, it is signed "Paul Reading, Narrow Lake, June, 1927."

The early brass fly reel has a folding ivory handle and a raised rear click housing; the foot is drilled to lash on a leather drag pad.

THE LARGE creel, woven of varnished whole (not split) willow strips, is of center-hole design; its straps and fittings, not shown, are thought to be original. The small creel is a center-hole, split-willow brook trout basket; the narrow hole marks it as an early type.

The wood & brass British "Nottingham" reel, stamped "Allcock & Co," has bone handles and a starback frame with a click button and a wire line guard.

A CHRISTMAS morning scene, 26x20 inches, attributed to a Fred Craft. As it is a black-and-white oil painting, it was probably commissioned as an illustration for a sporting magazine.

AN UNUSUAL promotional display. The illustration is oil on canvas, signed by Albert Fisher (lower left); the Kingfisher billboard is a separate piece overlaid on the painting.

THERE'S MORE *to life—and to collecting—than mere fishing tackle.*
This oil painting on canvas is signed by Bill Kroening. It has an
unmistakable air of promotional display to it.

HEDDON'S DOWAGIAC
RODS AND MINNOWS

1910

THE JAMES HEDDON & SONS catalog for 1910, photographed by
Clyde A. Harbin, Sr.

"THE FISHERMAN," by George Bellows. *Point Lobos, California, June 1917. When the Berry-Hill Galleries of New York City bought the painting for $1.4 million, it set a new price record for a fishing subject— one that won't likely be broken at any tackle flea markets.*

THE LATE Ogden Pleissner, of Vermont, was a well-known painter of angling scenes. This one, of Atlantic Salmon fishing on the Restigouche River, is noted for being the first of his sporting works to be reproduced as a print.

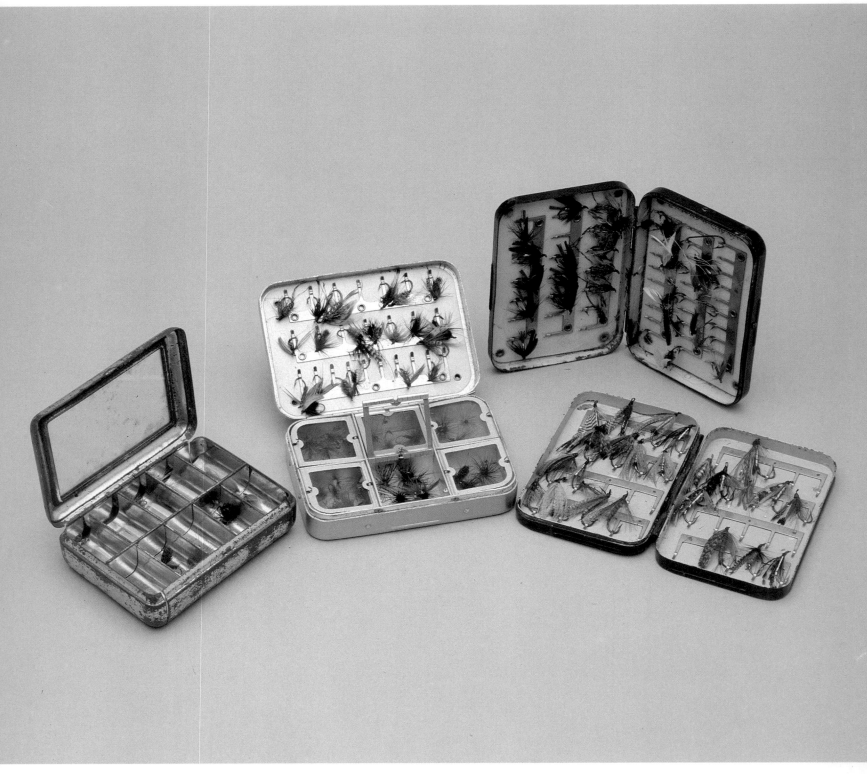

A FINE representative assortment of older fly boxes that are widely available at swap meets, flea markets and auctions. The 3 1/2x2 1/2-inch Wheatley fly box, with its individual compartment covers, is very similar to current models. The two black japanned tin boxes are handsome but unremarkable; the glass-topped box is more unusual. The trout flies are original.

ANGLING BOOKS are a collectible field unto themselves, and they are commonly mixed in with tackle at flea markets and sales.

THIS FINE copper "gut cast box" (right) with its hinged lid held a fly fisherman's casts, or leaders. The smaller of the other tins is cork-lined for fly hooks. The larger one (6 1/2x3x2 inches) has three compartments and another lid under its handsome embossed cover.

More "Spook" Bodied Fly Rod Lures

Transparent Bodies. Indestructible Construction. Very Buoyant.

Heddon "POPPER-SPOOK". No. 940 Series. A New Fly Rod Lure

No. 940 Series

4/5 Actual Size

Bass and pan-fish strike this little top-water fly rod lure. Body transparent, with cupped front, it can be made to bubble or pop by a short twitch of rod tip. Has colored hackle at its rear. Hook molded into body and held fast. Outlasts half a dozen cork-bodied lures. Casts easily and accurately. Length 1 1/8 in. Weight 1/25 oz. No. 5 hook. **Each, $ .60**

940GR	Grey Body, Grey Hackle
940WR	White Body, Red Hackle
940BW	Black Body, Black Hackle
940BR	Brown Body, Brown Hackle
940Y	Yellow Body, Yellow Hackle
940DG	Green Body, Green Hackle

940GR   940WR   940BW   940BR   940Y   940DG

New "BUG-A-BEE SPOOK". No. 960 Series

No. 960BR

4/5 Size

A small "spent-wing" bug that fools the wisest fish. Lies helpless on the water with wings extended. Length 1/2 in. Very light. Colors same as "Popper-Spook." No. 4 hook. **Each $0.60**

960GR	Grey Body, Grey Hackle	960BR	Brown Body, Brown Hackle
960WR	White Body, Red Hackle	960Y	Yellow Body, Yellow Hackle
960BW	Black Body, Black Hackle	960DG	Green Body, Green Hackle

No. 950 Series "RIVER-RUNTIE-SPOOK"

A Tiny Fly Rod Wiggler that fills a long-felt want. Also effective with cane pole.

No. 950 Series

4/5 Actual Size
Color 959XRY

Floats and dives a few inches under water, and wiggles like a small minnow. Excellent for Bass, Crappies, Bluegills, etc. Also large Trout. Weight 1/25 oz. No. 5 Model Perfect Hook. Hook moulded into body and cannot pull out. Length 1 1/4 in.

Each, $ .60

952	White and Red	959XRG	Green Shore-Minnow
959L	Perch Scale	959XRS	Silver Shore-Minnow
959P	Shiner Scale	959XRY	Yellow Shore-Minnow

On the "Runtie"
Muse Davis
Yazoo City, Miss.

Rainbows on "Runtie"
Chas. S. Hoffman, Jr.

Cork Bodied Fly Lures

No. 720 Series "FLAP-TAIL BUG" Liveliest of Surface Lures. A real swimming "Bug" that brings savage smashes.

Color 720Y

The tiny flapping spoon at tail gives a lifelike swimming action just like an insect swimming for its life. On a fast retrieve, the spoon breaks water, reverses its revolutions and kicks up a lot of surface commotion. An excellent caster and sure hooker for Bass, large Trout, etc. Length 1 1/4 in., weight 1/25 oz. No. 1 size hook.

No. 720WR	White and Red	No. 720BR	Brown
No. 720Y	All Yellow	No. 720GM	Grey Mouse
No. 720GR	Grey		

Each, $ .60

Note: The "Mouse Flap-Tail" has ears, beady eyes and fur-finish. Very lifelike.

Heddon "POP-EYE FROG". No. 85 Series. (Fly Rod Lure)

No. 85 Series

85GF

There is something in the tantalizing stare of the downward-looking popping eyes that makes Mr. Bass really mad. "The Eyes have IT." Casts nicely, easy pick-up and never turns over. Equipped with effective weed-guard. Cork body, bucktail legs. Length 3 1/2 in. Weight 1/20 oz.

85YF	Yellow and Black Frog	85GF	Green and Black Frog

Each, $ .85

[40]

OLD TACKLE catalogs are frequently as sought-after as their merchandise. Along with being authentic collectibles themselves, they also help identify and date tackle, and they are important chapters in the history of fishing. This is page 40 of the 1939 Heddon Catalog, photographed by Clyde A. Harbin, Sr.

COLLECTOR'S GUIDLINES

AN ANTIQUE is not necessarily collectible; a collectible is not always or automatically an antique. We have got it in our heads that anything in limited quantity, new or old, is desirable—*must* be so, because only relatively few people can possess these things, be they Seamaster reels, Ferrari roadsters or Dewey campaign buttons.

Sometimes this is in fact the case; often it is not.

Entrepreneurs take advantage of our national mania for collectibles (and for nostalgia) with mass-market made-to-be-rare merchandise, in a phenomenon that we might call the Franklin Mint Syndrome. They sell their wares through advertisements that solemnly promise "the molds will be destroyed" and the production "strictly limited." Caveat emptor, for many of these items should never have been created in the first place, and the production runs may be limited only by the number of orders they receive. The flood of junk "collectibles" is lapping around our ankles and threatening to rise higher.

To date, no tackle makers have succumbed to this syndrome, and the few reels and rods and the like that have been intentionally gussied up for the collectibles market (often for fishing-club fund raisers, with special cosmetics or serial numbers) are in fact completely fishable and rather desirable. But how long can it be before a lure company reaches into its archives and reissues a wooden-bodied classic from the 1940s, decorative box and all—with an owner-registration card and the promise of rapid appreciation? Fishing tackle will then have crossed an important line, from functional utility to mere decoration.

The more established manufacturers of collectibles can (and do, over and over) point with pride to a handful of their items that, in the span of one or two decades, did in fact appreciate in dollar value.

This is no guarantee their current offerings will do the same. From the early 1970s to the late '80s, the Consumer Price Index, a measure of inflation, has about tripled. So don't be impressed that a commemorative dinner plate, for example, that sold for $10 then might bring $30 today. That's simply keeping up with the times. Anything beyond that may–*may*–be real gain.

TACKLE collectors with an eye for cash value may follow two routes: Visit auctions, flea markets and dealers in search of already old but undervalued fishing gear; or acquire new tackle that will appreciate, and faster than the cost of living.

Identifying contemporary items today that will be valuable antiques tomorrow is almost as difficult as picking the right stock on Wall Street, and many of the same rules apply, beginning with that cornerstone of capitalism, Supply and Demand. (How many of those plates–or wrist watches, or tackle catalogs–were actually made? How good are they? How many might survive?)

There is an easy, almost foolproof way to build such a tackle "portfolio," but it requires a healthy outlay of cash and some patience. In the same way that shares in established blue-chip stocks can generally be counted on to grow in value over time, money put into certain top-line contemporary fishing gear can *probably* be considered a true investment. Today, that means ordering expensive split-bamboo fly rods or handmade fly reels from the recognized maestros and waiting one to three years, or longer, for delivery.

(With the possible exception of offshore big-game fishing with its high-cost, low-volume trolling reels, today only fly-fishing offers this sort of modern tackle masterpiece. New fishing-related art-work–paintings, carvings, bronzes and the like–is another matter, subject in part to the standards and unofficial rules of the fine arts market.)

When it arrives, you will have an example of craftsmanship that can be fished with great pleasure, displayed or sold at a gain. Naturally, it has to be cared for properly, but compared to a vintage Due-senberg or a French Impressionist painting, maintenance and insurance for fishing tackle are virtually no-cost.

On the other hand if, as some tackle collectors and most players in the stock market do, you want to buy low today and sell high tomorrow, you have to learn the field inside and out. You should also stick to a few basic rules and   develop a gambler's hunches for when to break those rules.

It's safe to say that the fishermen who bought Riley Haskell's copper minnow lures for pennies around the time of the Civil War had no idea that one would sell for $22,000 a century and a quarter later. A few of those fishermen might have admired the first-rate workmanship of the lures and, prompted also by the relative scarcity of such tackle then, might have cared for them a bit better than they did for some other things. And it may be that the dozen or so Haskell minnows known to exist today belonged to those fishermen. If so–but in reality, sheer dumb luck likely had a lot more to do with the survival of those lures–that's approaching the sort of prescience I'm talking about, the ability to zero in on tomorrow's collectible today, before its admirable qualities become evident to others.

FOR WHAT they're worth, I offer the rules I try to operate by when examining angling collectibles, contemporary or vintage, to keep or to resell:

1. Is it well made? You don't need to be a mechanical engineer to spot quality; in fishing tackle, your

eyes and your fingers can tell you much.

2. Is it an original? The real thing? If appropriate, is it signed or otherwise marked by the maker? This can apply to bamboo rods or ice-fishing decoys as well as to angling posters, prints or paintings.

3. Is it in good condition, considering its approximate age?

4. Are all the components there? Rods should be in their original bags or tubes or forms; better reels have always come in boxes or cases and with instruction sheets, some with tools or spare spools. A set of books or magazines should be complete. Any lure is more interesting in its box. And original sales slips or price tags are frosting on the collector's cake.

5. Did it belong to anyone significant? If so, does it bear his or her signature, initials, personal crest? Is the item mentioned in a letter, book or magazine article of its day? To a professional, significant owners might be Zane Grey, Bing Crosby or any of our many fishing presidents, to name a few. To the private collector, a significant owner might have been Uncle Bob who taught him to fish.

6. Is the provenance credible? Provenance is a collectible's pedigree, the proof that it is what its owner claims it to be. It's possible to fake almost any sort of documentation, and the higher the price of the item, the greater the motive for dishonesty. As the antique tackle market expands, so will the business of manufacturing antique tackle.

Anyone who pays thousands of dollars for, say, a Theodore Gordon dry fly had better be satisfied with its provenance, recognizing that a skilled modern fly dresser with a stash of the correct tying material could turn out a duplicate. (Gordon died in 1915, so he can't be reached for confirmation. And flies, unlike Packards or Winchesters, bear no serial numbers.) There are ways to age a contemporary fish decoy to make it look like a weatherbeaten centenarian. To properly counterfeit certain antique fishing reels might be too expensive to be worthwhile, but engraving "A. LINCOLN" onto a genuine but otherwise unremarkable Kentucky baitcasting reel might prove profitable.

Curiously, building a brand new famous old name bamboo rod can be surprisingly simple. The tapers, tools and engraving stamps, the line guides and wrapping thread, and even some of the raw bamboo of several of the old masters have been acquired by modern split-cane rod builders. With their skills, they could easily create new-old H.L. Leonards, for example, or maybe Jim Paynes from the same materials and with the same tools as the old ones—only the hands and eyes (and perhaps the serial numbers) would be new and "fake." To a man, fortunately, these rod craftsmen are too fiercely proud to commit such impieties, and the quick buck artist has neither the skills nor the equipment, we hope.

Provenance boils down to being expert enough to make a judgement oneself, or relying on the word and reputation of the person who's doing the selling.

My final, and sometimes most important, criterion is this: Whatever the thing is, do I just plain like it? Do I like it enough to pay its price happily, or to try to haggle the price down? Might I display it with pride at home, or even use it with pleasure on the water? Provenance, resale value, estimated rate of appreciation and all that matter much less then.

If I can answer "yes" to these questions (most of them, anyway, and particularly the last one), then it's perfectly all right to make a purchase, budget permitting.

ALL THIS is pretty grim stuff, for which I feel nearly compelled to apologize. Clearly, a growing number of people earn a satisfactory and enjoyable living dealing in collector-quality tackle, and if they rely on this trade to put Junior through college and food on the table, then it can become serious. The rest of us, however, should remember that enjoyment is supposed to be come first—we are pursuing Truth & Beauty, not just dollars. While it's normal to feel an added glow at acquiring something good at a bargain price, the value of a collectible to the amateur is determined only by how much he or she paid for it (instead of how much it might resell for), and what its craftsmanship or history mean to us emotionally. Within reason, dollars should matter mostly to our insurance carriers.

"THE BASSMAN," Clyde Harbin, Sr., of Memphis, Tennessee, with a small part of his collection of lures. He is holding the rare and valuable James Heddon Wooden Frog seen elsewhere in this book.

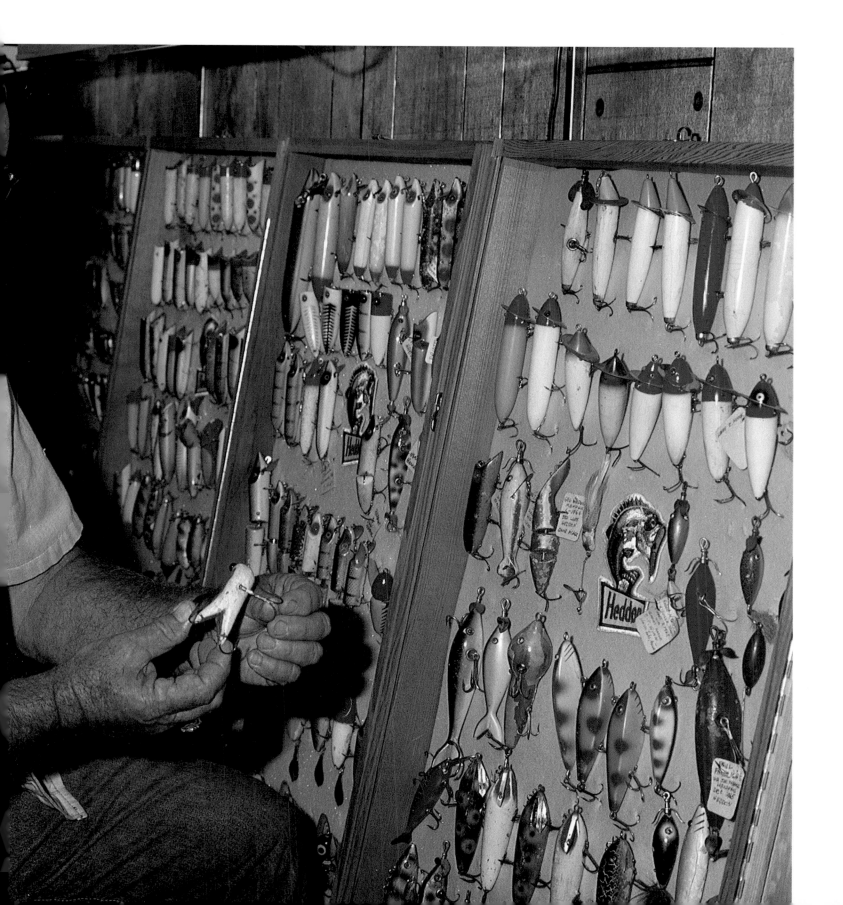

A WELL-STOCKED tackle swap meet can offer a bewildering assortment of merchandise. Clearly, in a situation like this, "knowledge is power."

A VINTAGE tackle swap meet takes place every summer, concurrently with the RWO Classic Tackle Auction, in Kennebunk, Maine.

SOURCES

Richard W. Oliver Auction Gallery
P.O. Box 337
Kennebunk, ME 04043

Richard A. Bourne Auction Gallery
P.O. Box 141
Hyannis Port, MA 02647

Fishing Lure Collector's Club
Larry Smith
3907 Wedgewood Drive
Portage, MI 49008

BIBLIOGRAPHY

Many of these titles are currently out of print and available only from dealers in sporting books—they have become, in fact, angling collectibles themselves.

American Fly Fishing—A History
Paul Schullery
(New York: NLB 1987) 278 pages. Index, bibliography, notes, b&w photographs, prints and drawings. $29.95 hardcover.

The American Sporting Collector's Handbook
Allan J. Liu, editor
(Piscataway, NJ: Winchester Press, rev. ed. 1982) 369 pages. Index, bibliographies, b&w photographs. Hardcover. Out of print.

Antique Fishing Reels—"Your illustrated guide to identifying and understanding U.S. patented models through 1920"
Steven K. Vernon
(Harrisburg, PA: Stackpole Books 1985) 192 pages. Index, patent list, b&w diagrams and photographs. $19.95 hardcover.

The Art of the Atlantic Salmon Fly
Joseph D. Bates, Jr.
(Boston: David R. Godine 1987) 232 pages. Index, bibliography, b&w drawings and photographs, 25 color plates. $65 hardcover.

Classic Rods and Rodmakers
Martin J. Keane
(Stockbridge, MA: Classic Publishing Co. 1976, 1983) 246 pages. Index, color and b&w photographs, b&w drawings and diagrams. Hardcover. Out of print.

A Collector's Reference Guide to Heddon Fishing Lures
Clyde A. Harbin, Sr. and Bill Wetzel
(Bill Wetzel, Box 1027, Bamberg, SC 29003) 56 pages. Heddon lure rating and appraisal system. $17 ppd.

Early Fishing Plugs of the U.S.A.
Art and Scott Kimball
(Boulder Junction, WI: Aardvark Publications, revised ed. 1989) Approx. 232 pages. Index, bibliography, b&w photographs, color plates. Hardcover $38.

The Encyclopedia of Fishing Lures
Loring D. Wilson
(San Diego, CA: A.S. Barnes & Co., Inc. 1980) 350 pages. Index, manufacturers' directory, b&w photographs. $19.95 hardcover.

Favorite Flies and their Histories
Mary Orvis Marbury
(Secaucus, NJ: The Wellfleet Press, 2nd modern reprint 1988) 522 pages. Indices, b&w photographs and drawings, 32 color plates. $17.95 hardcover.

The Fine Bamboo Fly Rod—"A Master's Secrets of Restoration and Repair"
Stuart Kirkfield
(Harrisburg, PA: Stackpole Books 1986) 191 pages. Index, b&w photographs. $29.95 hardcover.

The Fish Decoy—Vol. I & II
Art, Brad and Scott Kimball
(Boulder Junction, WI: Aardvark Publications 1986, '87) Vol. I 184 pages; Vol. II 192 pages. Indices, bibliographies, b&w photographs and color plates. $30 each.

Fishing Flies and Flytying
William F. Blades
(Harrisburg, PA: Stackpole Books ltd. facsimile ed. 1979) 319 pages. Index, b&w photographs and drawings, 5 color plates. Out of print.

Fishing from the Earliest Times
W. Radcliffe
(New York: Burt Franklin 1921, 1969) 478 pages. Index, b&w drawings and reproductions. Hardcover. Out of print.

Fishing Reel Patents of the United States 1838-1940
Jim Brown
(Stamford, CT: Trico Press 1986) 108 pages. Index, bibliography, b&w photographs, diagrams and drawings. $25 hardcover; edition limited to 350.

Fishing Tackle for Collectors
Charles Kewley and Howard Farrar
(New York: Sotheby Publications/Harper & Row 1987) 160 pages. Index, appendices, color and b&w photographs and plates, b&w drawings and diagrams. $39.95 hardbound.

Fly Reels of the House of Hardy
Glenn Stockwell
(London: Adam & Charles Black 1978) 58 pages. Index, b&w illustrations. Out of print.

Fly Reels of the Past
John Orrelle
(Portland, OR: Frank Amato Publications 1987) 155 pages. Bibliography, Index, notes, b&w photographs, drawings and diagrams. $19.95 hardcover.

Great Fishing Tackle Catalogs of the Golden Age
Sam Melner and Hermann Kessler
(New York: Crown 1972) Out of print.

A History of the Fish Hook
Hans Jørgen Hurum
(English ed: London: A.C. Black Ltd. 1977) 148 pages. Black-and-white and color photographs, drawings and diagrams. Hardbound. Out of print.

James Heddon's Sons Catalogs
The Bassman (Clyde A. Harbin, Sr.)
(Memphis, TN: CAH Enterprises. 1977) 326 pages. Reprints of entire 1903, 1907, 1919 and 1921 catalogs; b&w photographs, 12 color plates. 304 published. Out of print.

A Master's Guide to Building a Bamboo Fly Rod
Everett Garrison with Hoagy Carmichael
(Piscataway, NJ: Nick Lyons Books/Winchester Press 1985) 296 pages. Index, tables, b&w photographs, drawings and diagrams. $29.95 hardcover.

McClane's New Standard Fishing Encyclopedia and International Angling Guide
A.J. McClane, editor
(New York: Holt, Rinehart and Winston; rev. ed. 1974) 156 pages. Bibliography, tables, b&w and color photographs, drawings and diagrams.

Michigan's Master Carver—Oscar W. Peterson 1887-1951
Ronald J. Fritz
(Boulder Junction, WI: Aardvark Publications 1987) 104 pages. Color plates. $60 hardcover.

Old Fishing Lures and Tackle—"An identification and value guide"
Carl F. Luckey
(Florence, AL: Books Americana; 2nd ed. 1986) 371 pages. Index, b&w photographs, drawings and diagrams; 6 color plates. $14.95 softcover.

The Orvis Story—"Commemorating the 125th anniversary of The Orvis Company"
Austin Hogan, Paul Schullery
(Manchester, VT: The Orvis Co. 1980) 93 pages. Index, references, b&w photographs and drawings.

Streater's Reference Catalog of Old Fishing Lures
R.L. Streater
(Seattle: Rainier Press 1978) 441 pages total, including 1982 supplement. Index now being compiled; b&w reproductions of mfr's advertisements, catalog pages, and lures. $65 looseleaf format, with binder. Available from the author, Box 393, Mercer Island, WA 98040.

VIDEOTAPES
Antique Lures and Collectibles—An Overview
Antique Lures—Over 40 of the Rarest Antique Lures
The Heddon Collection
Antique Lures—The Heddon/Stokes Heritage
Phil Smith Productions and Clyde A. Harbin, Sr.
(Antique Lures, P.O. Box 154087, Irving, TX 75015) Approx. 60 minutes running time each. $29.95 plus $2 s&h each; $99.95 plus $3 s&h for the four-tape set.

INDEX

Accessories, 171-180, *181-210*, 211-214
  Fisherman's Knife, 175
  Fish Priests, 174
  Fly-Tying Vises, 178
  Gaff, 171, 176
  Landing Nets, 176
  Scale Knife, 176
  Waders, 177
B.D. Welch Tackle Company, *26*
Buel, Julio, 101, *121*
Carlson, Sam(Clarence H.), 16
Carpenter, Walt, 16, *44, 49, 50*
Casting, 54, 55
Chubb, Thomas, *37*
Collector's Guidelines, 211-214, *214-218*
Coxe, J.A., 60, *91, 96*
Creme, Nick, 56, 103
E.F. Payne Rod Manufactory, 16, *37*, 58, *81*, 213
F.E. Thomas Company, 16
Fin-Nor, 60
Fish Decoys, 147-152, *152-170*, 213
  Floater, 149
  Foodfish, 148, 149
  Ice, 151, 213
  New York, 148, *154, 155, 162, 170*
  Predatory, 149
  Real, 148
  Same-Kind, 149
  Spearing, 149, *155, 163*
  Sturgeon, 149
  Wooden, 148-151, *163-165*
  Working, 148, 151
Gordon, Theodore, 105, *108*, 213
Grey, Zane, 51, 59, 60, 88, *91*, 96, 98, 213

Harbin, Clyde, 105, *214*
Hardy Uniqua, *33, 89*
Heddon, James, 102, *129-141*, 151, *201, 210, 214*
Hofmeister, Russ, 106
Jordan, Wes 17
Keane, Martin, 15
Kovalovsky, Arthur, 60, *88*
Kovalovsky, Oscar, 60, *96*
Landing Nets, 176
Leonard, Hiram, 12, 16-18, 58, *81, 83*
  H.L. Leonard Company, 16, *81*, 213
Lures, 105, 106, *107-146, 214*
  British Phantom Minnow, 101
  Comstock Flying Helgramites, 101, *114*
  Haskell Minnow, 101, 105, *113*, 171, 212
  Hawaiian Wiggler, 103
  Hula Popper, 103
  Jitterbug, 103
  Muskie, 103, *115, 121*
  Pikie Minnow, 102, *146*
  Vivif, 104
McClane, A.J., 52
Montague Rod Company, *37*
Nottingham "Wynche," 52
The Orvis Company, 10, 17, 58, *184*
Peterson, Oscar, 150, 151, *152-155, 157-159*
Philbrook, Francis J., 58
Phillipe, Mitchell, Murphy & Greene, 42
Powell, E.C., *29*
Reels
  Automatic, 60, 64
  Baitcasting(Spinning), 51-57, 59, 61, 65-67, 75, 78, 79, 172
  Billinghurst, 57, 58
  Big-Game, 51, 57, 60, *91*, 96

Bogdan, 59, 61, 92, 95, 98
Brass, 72, 76, 84, 89, 195
  Center-Spindle, 53
  "Classic" Raised-Pillar, 58
Click-Type, 53, 54
Coxe, 38
Fly, 51, 53, 54, 57-60, 61, 64, 69, 76, 80, 85, 87, 89, 95, 181,
      195, 212
  Free-Spool, 54
Gem, 57, 59, 82
Hardy Bros. 37, 59, 60, 64, 172, 181, 184
Indiana, 59
"Ivoroid," 42
Kentucky, 52, 54, 65-69, 213
  Leonard-Mills, 58
  Malloch's Spinning, 55, 56, 79
  Meek Bluegrass, 39, 54, 68, 71
  Meisselbach, 60
  Mitchell, 56
  Multiplying, 53, 54, 59, 84, 86, 92
  New York, 54, 72
Nottingham, 53, 54, 65, 196
  Offshore, 60
Orvis CFO, 54, 58, 80
Raised- Pillar, 42, 58, 81, 83, 181
  Raised-Pillar Trout Fly, 37
Salmon, 50, 59, 61, 64, 70, 83, 86, 87, 92, 97, 181
Saltwater, 89, 97
  Seamaster, 60, 61, 211
  Thread Line Spinning, 56
Trolling, 51, 57, 59, 60, 61, 88, 212
Trout, 51, 61, 65, 82-85, 91, 95
  Winch-Type, 57
  Winans & Whistler, 55
Rods
  Advanced Composite Materials, 18, 19
  "Amabilis," 38, 42

Millwards, 34
Multipiece, 11, 13, 14
"One of One," 42
One-piece, 13
Pack, 22, 29
Salmon, 50
"Sans Noeud," 42
  Sapling, 7
  Wooden, 11, 18, 25
Snyder, George, 54
Thomas & Thomas Rod Company, 38, 41, 42, 47
Vernon, Steven 54
Vom Hofe, 30, 33, 34, 58, 59, 64, 70, 71, 85, 86, 89, 96
Walker, Arthur, 59
Antique, 8
Bait, 10, 38
Bamboo, 15, 17, 19-21, 29, 38, 42, 44, 58, 171, 212, 213,
  "Blowline," 11
Cane, 7, 12, 13, 15-18, 20-21, 37, 38, 42, 44, 49, 171, 213
Carpenter Trout, 50
Casting, 9, 11
  Catskill Legend, 42
"Chicago," 10
  Dapping, 10
F.E. Thomas, 33, 34
  Fiberglass, 18, 19, 56
Fly, 11, 33, 37, 38, 42, 212
"Fountainhead," 42
Garrisons, 34
Goodwin Granger, 33
Graphite, 12, 18, 19
H.L. Leonard, 25, 30, 34
  "Isaak Walton," 29
Kosmic, 16, 22, 29, 42
L.L. Bean's "99," 17
Meisselbach "Catucci," 33